The Creative Family

The Creative Family

how to encourage
    imagination & nurture
family connections

text and photographs by

Amanda Blake Soule

illustrations by Betsy Thompson

 TRUMPETER · Boston & London · 2008

Trumpeter Books
An imprint of Shambhala Publications, Inc.
Horticultural Hall
300 Massachusetts Avenue
Boston, Massachusetts 02115
www.shambhala.com

9 8 7 6 5 4 3 2 1

First Edition
Printed in Singapore

♾ This edition is printed on acid-free paper that meets
the American National Standards Institute Z39.48 Standard.
Distributed in the United States by Random House, Inc.,
and in Canada by Random House of Canada Ltd

Designed by Lora Zorian

LIBRARY OF CONGRESS CATALOGING-IN-PUBLICATION DATA

Soule, Amanda Blake.
The creative family: how to encourage imagination and nurture
family connections/ Amanda Blake Soule.—1st ed.
    p.   cm.
ISBN 978-1-59030-471-6 (pbk.: alk. paper)
1. Handicraft. 2. Creative activities and seat work.
3. Family recreation. 4. Creative ability in children. I. Title.

TT157.S636 2008
745.5—dc22
2007030147

Dedicated to *Adelaide, Ezra, Calvin* and *Steve*

Logic will get you from A to B.
Imagination will take you everywhere.

—Albert Einstein

contents

acknowledgments

To Linda Roghaar, my agent, for sharing her wisdom, patience, fore-sight, and humor.

To Jennifer Brown, my editor extraordinaire, for making this process truly a pleasant one; and to everyone else at Trumpeter Books for their belief in and dedication to this project.

To Betsy Thompson, illustrator and friend, for sharing not only her beautiful art but her family as well.

To all the blog writers and readers of SouleMama, who inspire and encourage me every day.

To Jessie and Rachael, for their everyday encouragement, love, and laughter.

To Judy, for her open home, heart, and spiritual guidance.

To my family—Bethany, Michelle, Katie, Mom, and Dad—whose support, love, and sense of adventure with my little ones made it possible for me to write.

To Dorothy, my Nana, for sharing her talent and love of the craft; and to Mildred, my Meme and first reader, for her gentle and loving roots in which to flourish.

To my children, who teach me so much each and every day simply by being who they are: Calvin, for stretching, challenging, and inspiring me more than I thought possible; Ezra, for reminding me to imagine, dream, and laugh every single day; Adelaide, for the joy, strength, and light that she shines.

And my deepest thanks to Steve, an amazing papa, my dearest friend, my balance, and my rock.

Thank you all for the many ways you have made this book possible, and my life richer.

In gratitude.
—*Amanda*
May 2007

The Creative Family

introduction

A Creative Journey

At the heart of every mindful and loving family lie the seeds of endless creativity. With patience, support, and just a bit of guidance, that creativity can flourish and grow in beautiful ways. In our modern lives, it's all too easy to get swept up in the busyness of the day-to-day—meals, cleaning, school, work, and other life details often stand in the way of the time we need to pursue our creative endeavors. As parents, it is both our responsibility and our privilege to be sure that our family's creative spirits have all the room and tools they need to soar freely.

Fortunately, we don't have to "teach" our children to be creative—inherent in the very core of children's beings is the embodiment of creativity. To think of something in a new way, to inquire about something that others don't even question, to come up with something truly unique and new is what children do best. When we give our children the space and encouragement to explore their own creativity, they can become our most inspiring of artists, our most inquisitive of scientists, and our most original of philosophers.

As their parents, we are blessed to have these amazing teachers. I'm reminded of this each and every day as I watch my children in the simple and small, but fully creative and dynamic, things they do: Adelaide, our one-year-old, finding pure delight in a basket of fabric from which she can recover her favorite piece of purple silk and start a game of peekaboo; Ezra, our three-year-old, lying on a riverbank and examining handful after handful of the earth's rich clay, which he later portrays in a painting; Calvin, our five-year-old, rushing out of bed to draw his dream before he forgets it—a gigantic half-pipe with a dozen or so skateboarders, kids on scooters, and in-line skaters spinning around in circles, all with gigantic smiles on their faces. These seemingly simple acts of childhood are small, yet full of wonder, appreciation, and imagination.

Given the creative nature of children, it is no coincidence that so many of us are led to seek a more creative life in their presence. Either an old creative passion or pursuit that has been forgotten is internally churned up, or we suddenly feel a need for something else in our lives when we've never considered ourselves creative before. Being around even the youngest children—and the purity of their rich creative energy—brings out our need for that same innovative spirit. They inspire us not only to nurture and embrace all of who they are, but to nurture and embrace our own creative selves as well.

For me, my creative spirit was awakened—and awakened loudly— through the presence of my shining children and the lessons I've learned from them. As a child, I never would have defined myself as "creative," nor do I think my parents or teachers would have done so. I thought *creative* meant something much different—something having to do with skill and talent and "art." Surely, I would not fit into that category. In school, I stumbled my way through art classes, managing to do just enough to get by. In high school, during the one semester that home economics was required, I came one pillow project away from my first failing grade. I would make things here and there; I just never thought of that as "creating."

I would often make things with my paternal grandmother on the weekends. She was an accomplished seamstress and knitter, and my visits with her would start with a trip to the fabric store for a pattern and materials. More often than not, I would return home at the end of the weekend with a new garment that we'd made to-gether. I learned from her the skills of sewing, and I enjoyed our time together immensely, but I was never thrilled or passionate about the projects. In fact, I was rather turned off by the details and confusing nature of all the "rules" of sewing by pattern.

Later on, in my college years, I would periodically dabble in one crafty project after another—trying to teach myself to knit, playing with clay or pottery, sewing an apartment curtain here or there. I en-joyed all of it, but it was never anything that stuck, and eventually, I would pack the sewing machine (or whatever the supplies of the moment were) back up and store them in the closet.

All of that changed for me in a life-altering way when I was pregnant with my first child. I found myself suddenly consumed with wanting to knit. Which is just what I did. I knit morning, noon, and night. I knit with a passion that surprised and changed me. There was something powerful happening when I was knitting for my little one. I felt peaceful and soothed and calmed, and at the same time, fully present in the moment. The simple act of wrapping some yarn around two sticks was repetitive, meditative. As I would knit a baby sweater, blanket, or hat, I felt as though each stitch car-ried my intent and thoughts of love for the child who would be wearing it. It was becoming something before my eyes. So I knit and knit, and when my hands tired of knitting, I embroidered and even-tually began sewing. It was truly a gift to me—a gift of connection to the past, of mindfulness, of intent.

I had long had a love of vintage textiles, a love that came from my maternal grandmother. When I was a child, we would go on many grand adventures together through rural Maine to yard sales and antique shops looking for "treasures." Even as a young girl, I was drawn to the textiles—old quilts, embroidered linens. Years later when I was discovering knitting, all of this made sense for the first time. These old objects that I had loved and the handwork that I was now loving were a connection to the past, a connection to women before me who had made such beautiful things. Their objective was one of practical reality—keeping their family warm and clothed. Yet, also in the process, their love came through as they created amazing works of art.

By the time my first child was born, I realized that my newly found creativity was too important to lose. I began to notice that when I was able to fit a bit of creating into my day, I was more centered, at peace, and fulfilled. All those things made me a calmer, more patient, and more mindful parent. My needs were getting met, and I was therefore able to meet the needs of my children even better. Creating quickly became an essential requirement. I was determined to find a way and time to make creativity a part of my life as a mother. Knitting was a pretty easy medium for that. I changed the projects I was working on to accommodate our daily lives. I kept baskets of knitting throughout the house, so if I ever had just a minute, I could easily grab my work and knit while my son played on the floor with me. I'd work on simpler projects that required a bit less of my attention. And I'd always travel with a project, in case there would be a moment I could claim for creativity. Yes, I would even knit at long stoplights.

I know that I am not the only one whose creative life was sparked by the birth of their children. I have talked to so many other people who felt the same need arise once they became parents and to people who are searching for ways to incorporate their creative passion into family life—parents who are inspired to create themselves after watching their young children's creative spirits growing and soaring. Whether you've been creating your whole life or have been inspired to do so since becoming a parent, there *are* ways you can incorporate creativity into your day-to-day activities. It may take some tweaking, a bit of juggling, lots of rearranging, and much patience, but I assure you, it can be done if the desire is strong enough. And it is worth it. A large part of nurturing a spirit of creativity comes from being mindful, slowing down, observing, and looking around you at the beauty and inspiration all around. We are blessed as parents to have the best teachers for this—our children. Stop and watch your children often. *Really* stop and watch, and you'll see them using such creativity in everything they do—a toddler picking dandelions, a young child making something out of blocks—they inherently work and play with creativity, intent, and imagination.

I now have a need and desire to create every day. It may be as simple as a walk with my three-year-old during which we find a pinecone to bring home and draw together, or it may be handwork on a quilt that I work on in solitude. In many ways, it doesn't really matter what the daily outcome is. What is so deeply important to my soul and the soul of my family is the act and the process of creating itself.

As my need to create things on my own has grown because of my children, so has my desire to create *with* my children. I see both my personal creative efforts and the act of engaging creatively with my children as being on the same continuum of creative living—they feed into each other. Being creative (in whatever capacity) is important: important to me, because I feel myself to be a more complete person when my creativity is expressed; important to my children, who witness adults growing, sharing, and learning creatively; and important to my family, who grow and connect by creating together. It is so important to me that my children not only see this creative pursuit and drive in action, but also that we do it together and that they fully know, love, and embrace their own creative selves. A lot of my time and energy goes toward making this happen—thinking of things for us to do together and visiting the issues of why I want us to do them together.

This book is the result of that labor, and I hope that it will speak to you and give you practical tips and ideas toward making creativity happen in your everyday life as a family. The joyful act of creating together can be positively magical and truly a gift for everyone. Much of our cultural energy is spent filling our minds, hearts, and time with things *outside* our families, as is evident in the smaller amount of time that families spend together and at home. There's a missing piece in this search for fulfillment—the piece that's home, connection, and heart. While all the external events and energy are wonderful, it is often forgotten that the home and family can be a tremendous source of balance, happiness, inspiration, and creativity. The experience of turning inward toward our family for creative fulfillment can be an amazing and powerful experience for the entire family—young and old.

A NOTE ON THE PROJECTS

The activities and ideas in this book are written for the creative family, with a focus on the following four elements:

Self—the discovery or continuance of your own creative passions and interests

Child—the development and nurturing of your child's growing, creative spirit

Family—the deepening of parent-child bonds through the acts of creating together

Community—the ways in which we can connect to others around us, in both our local and global communities, through the act of creative living

Living a creative life doesn't necessarily mean that your time is spent with paint, markers, and sewing machine. Perhaps those aren't of interest to your family, which doesn't mean you are not creative. Living a creative life does mean that you and your family seek ways to nurture your creative spirit in whatever ways please you. Living a creative life can encompass all areas of our family life—from our hobbies, to the way we connect with nature, to the ways we connect in our community, to the ways we celebrate our days together, and to the ways we celebrate each other. This book attempts to offer a wide range of ideas on living creatively.

All of the activities included in this book have in some way had a presence in my family's life. They are a collection of projects we have loved in the past, projects we are currently in the midst of, or projects that we are planning for the future. There is a wide range of ability levels required, and great variety in the creative mediums they use. None of them are intended to be firm and rigid ideas that must be conformed to. Don't be afraid to be, well, *creative* about your use of these activities in your own family. Start at the beginning and do a chapter each month or skip around to what interests you the most. Let your children flip through the book, choosing a photograph that most appeals to them. Just find something that speaks to you and get started creating with or for your children.

My great hope in writing this book is that something you read here will spark a project in your family—and that fun will be had, connections will be made, and creative spirits of all ages will soar. The most important lesson I think we can learn is simply to create. Let your children see you creating. Create for yourself and for them. And create with them. When you do this with love and intent, I promise you there will always be beautiful results.

part one

Gathering

1

Preparing your
Creative Mind

One way to open your
eyes is to ask yourself,
"What if I had never
seen this before? What if I knew I would
never see it again?"

—Rachel Carson

The most important, and perhaps most obvious, factor in nurturing your children's creative lives is to model a creative life yourself. Chances are, if you've picked up this book, you already have a creative passion or hobby that you love or you simply love creating with your children. Perhaps there is something that inspires you, motivates you, and speaks to you. This hobby may be something that you've always done, that you can't imagine living without. Perhaps your creative passion is even your profession. Or maybe you're a creative hobby jumper, with your hands in a few different projects at once, or someone who changes hobbies every few years. The challenge for you, especially as a parent, is finding the time, energy, and space to continue your creative passions and ways to share your love of creating with your children.

Maybe you don't think of yourself as being "creative" at all. Or you haven't found that special something that calls you to create yet. Perhaps you are looking for ways to incorporate more creative activity into your lives. Now, my friends, is the time to nurture your creative side. If you need an excuse, let's call it a "job responsibility" that comes with parenting, okay? Nurturing your own creative spirit will not only bring more peace, satisfaction, and joy into your life and the lives of those around you, but it will also serve as a guide and model to your children on finding *their* creative selves. It's required. There. Now, you need to begin the search for that special something that will inspire you to create. Maybe it's something new that you've discovered, something you'd like to start doing, or something you've always secretly wished you could have done. Think back to what you loved in childhood, and forget what anyone might have said about your "skill" or "talent" (or lack thereof), and try to remember what you *liked* to do, what made you happy. Drawing? Painting? Doodling? Take a stroll through your local bookstore or library, browse through the shelves, and look for something that grabs you. Woodworking? Scrapbooking? Gardening? Think about the people in your life you think of as creative. Does anything they do interest you? Pottery? Piano? Guitar? Look through your local adult education catalog for ideas. Dance? Photography? Knitting? However you begin your search, the important thing is to begin. You're blessed with some amazing people to learn from in the development of your creative self—your children.

As parents, we are truly blessed to have in our lives both the most natural and intuitive "teachers" of creativity. I do believe that, as human beings, we are all born with the ability, the desire, the passion, and the drive to be creative. We may become anxious about "teaching" creativity to our children, but there is really no need for us to teach. They *know* how to be creative. They know it with every ounce of their being—it isn't conscious or rational. It is simply who they are. Until something stands in their way (I'm sure you know or can imagine the daily obstacles that some children face in their creative endeavors), they will be creative. Furthermore, if we are willing to open ourselves up to the possibility, our children can teach us how to be creative. It is imperative to keep this in mind: we are not their teachers on this journey. We can be their guides; their assistants; their facilitators; their researchers; sometimes their directors; and other times, their faithful, open, and patient students.

Before beginning any of the activities in this book, I encourage you to think about letting your child be the guide, director, and teacher, while you try to be a student. Your role is to provide the environment and to watch and learn. Try to forget and put aside all the things running around in your mind—all the lists that need completing, all the distractions of your day, and all the mess that you might be making (don't even think about the cleanup process yet). Focus on your child. Watch. Never forget to play (and if you've forgotten how, just watch your child).

As difficult as it may be to shift your thinking from that of adult responsibilities such as cleaning up, try as hard as you can to think a bit differently about your children's "messes." When your child stomps through a mud puddle, soaking his clothes and boots, try to think of the experience gained—the sensation of the water squishing between his toes. When your child slips her hands right into that puddle, think of the way she is touching the earth—getting a sense for how things change in the soil. All of their messes are really lessons about life and the earth. Don't be afraid to get dirty, and don't be afraid of the mess (if you're worried about stained clothing, try designating certain clothes just for messy play). Be in the moment as much as you possibly can, and follow your child's natural, creative imagination wherever it may lead you both. If the idea of this overwhelms you, put a time frame on the activity. Can you set a timer? Sometimes it helps (the adult) to become fully absorbed in the activity knowing that there is an end time—it's easier to be actively mindful for a short period of time at first.

In the process of allowing and encouraging the growth of our children's inherent creative spirits, we can also simultaneously heal, nurture, and grow our own. You'll soon discover that as your child blossoms and shines creatively, you will also uncover or expand your creative self more fully. It's a beautiful journey you're taking—with your child *and* yourself.

GRATITUDE

Wind

Maple syrup

Ketchup

Belly buttons

Cheese

Sunshine

Falling leaves

Gnomes

Castles

Ocean waves

—A few selections from a week of "lunchtime gratitudes"

Creativity goes deeper than the "art" sense of the word; it encompasses a whole way of living and being. Gratitude, and recognizing gratitude, can have a powerful effect on our whole lives. When we feel grateful, we feel full—full of love, full of inspiration, full of ideas, and full of creative spirit. Practicing gratitude in our families can help our children learn this power (one they have within themselves) at a young age, giving them a lifelong gift that will nurture all of who they are.

If it isn't something that we have thought of much as adults, practicing gratitude on a daily basis can take some practice and determination (especially if we are still "getting over" the way we were *forced* to show gratitude as children), but it's a practice well worth the effort, particularly for the little ones we're modeling for. There's a big difference between being forced to say, "thank you," and actually feeling genuine, authentic gratitude. I try to differentiate the two in our home (oftentimes this means saying thank you for my children as a way to model it without forcing it) and strive for the latter. The following are some ways to incorporate gratitude into your family's daily life.

Write Thank-You Cards

In our age of e-mail, it feels wonderful and special to receive a handwritten note, doesn't it? As much as possible, we make a point of sending thank-you cards, not just for gifts, but also for gestures of kindness, time, and love. I'm careful not to force this on my children, but to make it something they are motivated to be a part of. If they aren't in the mood, I wait a few days and try again, or I just do it myself without much of a fuss.

Usually, the thank-you card consists of a drawing by one of my little ones, with a few of their words dictated and handwritten by me. Another idea for small children is to have them do just one thank-you drawing, scan it into your computer (or photocopy it), and print it on paper or cardstock to make a set of cards. Like most "work" that we do as parents—cooking, cleaning, and washing—our children want to "play" like we do. So let your children see you sit down to write a few thank-you cards once in a while, and before you know it, they'll be at their own desks doing the same.

The Gratitude Alphabet

This can be so much fun and quite silly. On a large piece of paper, we write down the letters in the alphabet, then we go through them together and write down something we are grateful for that corresponds with each letter. It's amazing how, even in the context of silliness, the act of saying aloud so many things we are grateful for really does make us feel more aware of how full, loved, and blessed our lives truly are.

The Gratitude Hug

This is a little ritual in our house that sometimes has the power to heal hurt feelings or the ache of a bruised knee. When someone isn't feeling their best, one of the kids sometimes suggests doing a "talking hug," which is when we figuratively hug and shower the hurting one in gratitude, going back and forth and saying all the things we are grateful for about that person.

Daily Gratitude

Finding a way to incorporate gratitude into your daily life really can have tremendously transformative powers and do wonders for developing your little one's compassion. Try expressing a daily gratitude before or after your dinner blessing or before bedtime. They can be silly, fun, light, or serious, but they always feel good.

Thank Your Elders

And your peers and all the people around you. Take things a bit slower when you're out in the world so you have the time to say "thank you" with a smile. Say the things you're thinking. If you had really great service somewhere, don't just keep it to yourself. Say it! Most especially, find regular moments to thank those special older people in your life who taught you about so many things.

Thank Your Children

Yes, yes, yes! Don't forget that your little one needs thanks and gratitude very much. Simply because something is expected doesn't mean it shouldn't be recognized. Say, "thank you." And tell them you're grateful for them every single day.

Thank Yourself

Encourage your children to be grateful for themselves. What traits do they most appreciate about themselves? What traits do you most appreciate about yourself? Say, "thank you" for that every day!

Calvin's drawing and writing, scanned into the computer and printed onto cardstock for holiday Thank-You Cards.

INSPIRATION IS EVERYWHERE

Staying inspired is an integral part of living creatively and of creating itself. While there are times when we find inspiration everywhere and have no lack of ideas, concepts, or projects to try, there are other times when we need a little something to get us started. It's helpful to keep your eye out for inspiration and somehow save it for a time when you might need it. Feelings, thoughts, people, places, and moments are all full of inspiration that we keep in our hearts. But you can translate the idea of inspiration into a literal sense as well, as you begin to save bits of beauty that you find throughout your day. This is something you can do as an adult, something you can do as a family, and a part of the creative process that you can encourage in your children. Inspiration really is everywhere, and once your mind and eyes are open to look for it, you'll find beauty all around you. The following are some of the places we find the inspiration that we store up.

Magazines and Catalogs

When flipping through magazines, I often find many visuals that inspire me. The way two colors are blended together, a skirt I see on a child, the texture of a pillow, or a photograph of a beautiful place. I save these pages, not for duplication, but for inspiration later on. Sometimes the trim on a woman's dress in a magazine might be manifested in the edging of a pillow I make with the kids. I never know how what I cut out will end up being used, if at all. To avoid the cluttering trap of saving stacks of magazines to be pored through in the future, I rip out the pages that inspire me the first time I read through a magazine, so I'm never stuck trying to recall exactly where it was I saw something when I need it.

Old Books

One of my favorite sources for inspiration comes from vintage children's books. We love to find thrifted—that is, found at a thrift store—inexpensive, old children's books and use them in our craft projects. While many do make their way onto our bookshelves, others make their way to the craft table, particularly old books that are in poor condition, missing covers, and outdated. I love the design that is found in children's book illustrations from the 1950s and 1960s, and I will often clip those for inspiration. My children do the same, noting the different ways in which people draw and use color.

Kids' Art

Well, naturally! This is one of my favorite sources of inspiration, and I will often ask if I can keep a certain drawing on my Inspiration Wire (desribed later in this section) because I love the particular way my child has done something. I love the way their fresh, creative, and imaginative minds combine color, lines, and textures. They are so inspiring to me.

Other Paper Sources

Old wrapping paper, found cards, letters, vintage advertising, and newspapers are other paper sources that sometimes make their way onto our Inspiration Wire.

Textiles

Sometimes the color of a yarn will really grab me, and I'll clip a piece of that to my bulletin board. The same is true for bits of vintage fabric that I love but that are too small to work into a project. When I'm stuck on a project, these items might call me to try that color of yarn or to work in a bit of the design from the vintage fabric.

Photographs

My children's inspiration wall is usually full of photographs, as is mine. These include photos of moments, places, people, or objects that are beautiful and inspiring. Carrying a small camera around with you is perfect for those moments when you suddenly see lines in a building that represent something you'd like to incorporate into your creations later on. Take a photo, and keep it as your inspiration.

Now that you have all those inspiring pieces, you'll need to find a way to organize, save, and display them. Here are some ideas that have worked in our home.

Bulletin Board

An old standby is the classic bulletin board. A simple bit of cork-board can be a perfect way to store and see your saved bits of beauty and inspiration easily. This is particularly good for children, who can arrange and rearrange as they desire. To personalize your bulletin board, wrap a piece of fabric around it as you would wrap something with gift wrap, and staple the fabric to the wood on the back of the board frame.

Inspiration Wire

An Inspiration Wire is a great way to display your pieces anywhere. String a length of wire (with a screw or thumbtack on both ends) along a wall, door, or window. Then, using small clips or clothespins, hang up your inspirations just as if they were clothes drying on the line.

Folders

I keep my personal crafting inspiration bits in an accordion folder, divided and labeled according to the idea. Some of my folders are for children's clothing, design and color, home accessories, fabric, and so on. This makes it easy for me to find just what I'm looking for without being visually overstimulated in the middle of a project.

Whatever method you choose to display your inspiration, keep your collection accessible and visible in your family work and creating space (or your personal space, if they're your personal inspiration bits). Use your inspiration when you are looking for a new idea to try or a new direction to take. Your children will quickly grasp the idea of mixing and matching the bits of inspiration ("Oh! Let's make a puppet in *that* color, with *this* kind of a smile on it!"), and you'll all be on your way to recognizing and saving the bits of beauty you find everywhere in your lives.

Ezra works under our family inspiration wire, which holds an ever-changing collection of bits we find and are inspired by: nature, magazine clippings, and children's art and projects.

2

The most effective kind of education is that a child should play amongst lovely things.

—Plato

Gathering Materials

After finding the energy and spirit for nurturing a creative life, we now need the materials necessary for creation. It's important that these materials be chosen thoughtfully, appropriately, and mindfully. Having a decent supply of creative materials, or at least access to those materials, is an important message for our children (and a reminder to ourselves) that we take the "work" of creating seriously. Choosing quality over quantity, selecting supplies that we know our children will use, and having them all accessible are essential components to a creative home. This is all possible on a reasonable budget and in any size space.

The activities in this chapter will give you some ideas on how to get started choosing high-quality creative supplies for your family. It will also give you some concrete examples and patterns for materials you can make for and with your children.

USE THE GOOD STUFF

What you are going to read is not about spending more money. It is not about adding more stress to your role as a parent by needing more than you can afford. It is about how to choose high-quality materials for your children and how to treat those materials once you have them. The materials that we give our children to create with send them a message about how we value their creative endeavors, their time, and their work. When we care for and value their materials, so will our children. If we invest resources and treat the materials with respect, our children will know that their work is important to us. They will know we believe they are worthy of the "good stuff."

As adults immersed in our own hobbies, we enjoy working with high-quality materials, don't we? It's so much more satisfying to work on something when the materials you are using actually "work" and assist in what you are doing, rather than hinder and slow you down. The same should be applied to children's art supplies. Don't believe that because they are children, the materials should be inexpensive and the quality does not matter. They are going to be much happier painting with watercolors (or whatever the activity is at the moment) when the watercolor paints they have are absorbed into the paper well and won't fade with time. Go for quality over quantity; instead of having a box full of hundreds of decent crayons, buy fewer of the good-quality crayons. Visit your local art supply store and talk to the artists who work there. Ask how the materials work, ask to test them out, and see how they feel to hold. Would they be comfortable for little hands to use?

I encourage you to keep "family" art materials in your home, rather than separating your children's art supplies from your own. Let them know that all the materials are valued equally, and the adult materials aren't too good to be touched by children. The way you model the use, respect, and care of materials is what your children see and will hopefully embody.

You don't need a gigantic stock of art supplies for a successful creative home. We primarily work with colored pencils, crayons, watercolors, acrylic paints, and markers. When choosing materials, I look for products that are easy to use, resist smudging, and provide satisfying results. Add slowly to your collection as you are able, and share the excitement of new acquisitions with your children. They can be the best kinds of toys for the whole family.

Whether you have a big room dedicated solely to your creative projects or your kitchen table, it's important to create a space to store and use your family art materials. I dream about having a family studio in our home someday, but for now, the "studio" is also our dining room or our kitchen. Truth be told, I actually enjoy it this way. The creating that happens in our home takes place in our living space, not in a room with a door we can close. When we're eating our meals or gathering in the kitchen, we're surrounded by our work, making our creativity truly a part of our lives.

The biggest challenge with space is finding ways to keep our materials accessible, but still safe and out of the way when they aren't in use. In our dining room, we have a cabinet with doors that serves as our art cabinet. It's full of all our supplies, and having everything together makes it easy to dive into a project when inspiration strikes. For easy cleanup, I purchase inexpensive vinyl table-cloths at yard sales and thrift shops, which I also keep in the cabinet—ready to toss on the table for a quick painting or clay whim. This quickly transforms our dinner table into a safe-to-get-messy art space, and the vinyl makes it easy to wipe off and keep clean without additional laundry (because who wants that?).

A Note on Cost

"High-quality" materials don't necessarily mean "expensive" materials. We buy most of our art supplies at thrift stores, yard sales, or local art shops and schools that are getting rid of surplus. It takes a bit of extra effort to hunt down materials this way, but the results are worth it.

This cabinet—a "free" roadside find—keeps all of our art materials stored neatly in our dining room.

With the cabinet open, it quickly transforms our dining room into an art studio, with materials accessible for little hands.

Felt Pencil Roll

Give your children a special place to store their treasured art materials. This felt pencil roll can hold colored pencils, pens, or markers and is simple enough in construction that a child can make one with your assistance. This makes a lovely gift as well, for your child or for a friend. The pencil holder can be sewn by hand or machine. The dimensions given for this project will hold approximately twelve 7-inch-long pencils.

This simple to make felt pencil roll keeps pencils safely and compactly stored until drawing time.

What You'll Need

- Four pieces of felt cut to the following sizes: two pieces measuring 19 × 9 inches, one piece measuring 19 × 5 inches, and one piece measuring 19 × 2 inches (I prefer 100 percent wool felt, or a wool/polyester blend. Both are thicker than the standard polyester felt you might remember from your own childhood craft days. See the Resource Guide for assistance in locating felt.)
- Ribbon, approximately 24 inches in length
- Any embellishments you'd like: sequins, embroidery, buttons, patches, and so on
- Craft glue to attach embellishments
- Thread, needle, scissors, pins

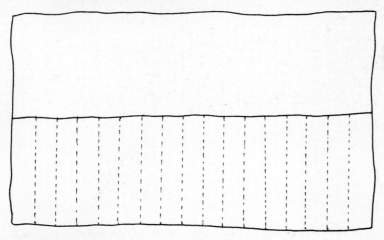

Illustration A.

What to Do

1. Place any embellishments you would like on one side
   of one of the larger (19 × 9 inches) pieces of felt.
   Use glue or a needle and thread to attach. This will
   be the outside of your roll. Put this piece aside until
   the last step.

2. Place the 19 × 5-inch piece on top of the second
   large (19 × 9) piece, lining up three sides.

3. Sew around the edges on these three sides. The open
   side will become your pencil pocket.

4. With chalk or a pencil, mark lines approximately one
   inch apart along the length of the felt pieces, on top
   of the pocket piece. (See illustration A.) Use your
   chosen pencils/markers as a guide to be sure they
   will fit, and adjust the measurements accordingly.

5. Stitch along these lines, making a "slot" for each
   pencil. (See illustration A.)

6. Now place the 19 × 2-inch piece of felt along the
   top of the pencil roll, and line it up along the three
   sides; sew around the edges of those three sides. This
   will create a "pocket" at the top so the pencils do not
   slip out of the roll.

7. Place your embellished piece of felt (the "outside" of
   the roll) flat, with the embellishments facing down.
   Pin the felt piece with pockets on top of this (pockets
   facing up), and line it up along all four sides. Sew
   these two pieces together. Trim the edges with scissors, using pinking shears if a more decorative effect

is desired, but being careful not to cut too close to the stitches.

8. Place the length of ribbon, folded in half, approximately halfway down one of the shorter sides of the back of the roll; sew the ribbon piece securely onto the roll (see illustration B). When the piece is rolled up, this will tie together, keeping the pencils secure.

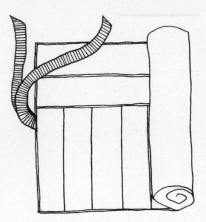

Illustration B.

THE BEST TOYS

Our lives today are full of more and more "stuff." The things we have around us and the things we see in our daily lives all greatly affect the way in which we create. Before you bring toys into your home, I encourage you to think about the following questions and apply them not only to new toys coming in, but the toys already in your home as well.

Is It Beautiful?

Do the tools and toys around you evoke a feeling of beauty? By choosing carefully what toys you bring into your home, you can encourage a love and appreciation for good design and craftsmanship. Choosing to surround ourselves with beautiful design can be a great source of inspiration. Choose toys that are handcrafted, when possible. Search out toys that feel good to touch and hold and are visually pleasing. Think beyond the big-box store for your children's toys and look to antique shops, thrift shops, your local woodworker, and "natural" toy catalogs (see the Resource Guide to get you started). Finding toys that will hold up to lots of use and play—versus poorly made toys that will break easily—will encourage your children to value human work and experience over consumption.

Is It Simple?

Many modern toys are sophisticated and technologically complicated, which certainly have their place and importance in our lives. But the downside is that they can often eliminate a need for imagination when playing. If there's a toy that does it all for you, there's little room left for creativity. Think about selecting toys that can be used in a multitude of ways and that evoke imagination and creative expression. Many classic, simple toys of the past are full of these creative possibilities. Look beyond the plastic dolls that "do everything" and head toward a simple cloth doll that can grow with a child or a big basket of wooden blocks that can be a toddler's stacking tower or a child's fort. Toys that grow with a child will encourage even more imaginative play; the way they use the toys will change over the years.

What Is It Made Of?

Can you tell how a toy is made? While there is certainly room and a need for some manufactured plastic in our lives, we also need to make much more room for simple, natural materials. Does your children's toy selection show an adequate representation of nature? Is there wood? Cloth? Natural fibers? Not only do these toys *feel* good to play with and connect children to the outside world, but they are also often strong enough to last a lifetime and even more. I think we should consider our toy materials in the same way that people talk about whole foods: the closer to the original source, the better. Can you picture your toy growing somewhere on the earth? Wooden blocks, felt balls, and cotton dolls are often some of the best toys. (See chapter 3 for ideas on making your own toys from natural materials.)

What Senses Does It Use?

Do the toys in your home evoke the use of many senses? We experience the world through our senses—with our ability to see, hear, feel, touch, and taste—and children are particularly sensitive to this as they discover the world with fresh eyes, ears, and so on. Try to include at least one toy in your home that represents each of the senses. And the ones that encourage play while using more than one sense? Even better!

How Is It Organized?

In our own adult creative lives, it helps the creative spirit tremendously when things are accessible, easy to find, and available. Beginning a project seems much less like a monumental feat when the materials are readily at hand. If too much time is spent looking for what you need, creativity often goes by the wayside. Keeping toys organized in baskets, boxes, and on shelves (all within easy reach for little ones) helps so that children know just where they are when inspiration strikes.

A primary source of play in our home, this child's kitchen is simple and natural in construction, and suited for various kinds of play for children of all ages.

Is There Too Much?

When it comes to playthings for our children, I can't emphasize enough that for creative play, *less really is more* in regard to toys. Between generous gifts from family members, hand-me-downs, and accessible inexpensive toys, it is quite likely that our homes are cluttered and full of playthings. A sad product of our modern world is that our children are taught early on to overconsume and to want more, more, and more. Chances are that they do not need more toys, but fewer. When there are too many things around, there's little room for imagination. Clean out some of the toys you have now that are not used often, and think more critically about the ones you let into your home. Tell family members your philosophy and ask them to share it when they make purchases for your children. Rotating toys in and out of the play space can also be a helpful way to use fewer at a time, and it can provide a "new" way of looking at an "old" toy.

Wool Felt Block

This block can be a first sewing project for a child or an adult, and it makes a wonderful gift for a baby. When stuffed with rice or millet instead of wool, it can become more like a Hacky Sack or juggling ball for an older child. (See chapter 6 for help on getting started with hand sewing.)

The pieces of a felt block, ready to be assembled by child or adult.

What You'll Need

- Wool felt pieces, approximately 20 inches square in total, in colors of your choosing (I prefer 100 percent wool felt or a wool/polyester blend felt. Both are thicker than the standard polyester felt you might remember from your own childhood craft days. See the Resource Guide for assistance in locating this type of felt.)
- Stuffing for the block (I like stuffing with wool or cotton, if it's available. Polyester stuffing will work too, however. If you are making this for a child (not an infant), millet or rice make for a sturdier block, more like a Hacky Sack or juggling ball.)
- Small bell for the inside of the block (optional)
- Needle, scissors, thread

What to Do

1. Cut out six 3-inch felt squares, using whatever color combination you like.
2. Begin sewing the sides of the square panels together (see illustration C). Any stitch will do, but the blanket stitch looks quite nice for this project.
3. Continue sewing the sides together to create a block, until you get to the last side. Leave this open and stuff the block firmly with the filling, so that it maintains its shape.

4. If you are inserting a bell, do so at this point.
5. Finish sewing the open side of the block.

Illustration C. Order of construction for the felt block.

3

Being Resourceful

The earth is what we all have in common.

—Wendell Barry

We all know that family life has changed dramatically in recent years. It wasn't all that long ago that things were different, and there's a likely chance that you have someone in your life—a grandparent, an elderly neighbor, a friend—who has shared with you the ways their lives were dissimilar to ours. My maternal great-grandmother, Florence, raised six children alone in rural Maine in the midst of the Depression. Like so many others of her generation, she was a resourceful and creative woman who cleverly found ways to care for her family with virtually no income. Their lives were full of love, adventure, and creativity, but not material belongings. The few things they did have were precious and hand-made, and they lasted for years and years. Nothing was thrown away, and everything was given new life as something else once its original purpose was complete. Clothes were made by hand, and once they had been worn, patched, and worn again beyond repair, they became something else altogether: buttons were removed for future projects; and fabric became doll clothing, a quilt, or a dishrag.

Handmade objects were a necessity. Creating things by hand was a necessity. Living a creative life was second nature and just the way things were. People back then may not have thought of the work they did as creative or artistic, but that is what we now consider the work they left behind. We treasure the old, handmade quilts, sewing, and needlework, as well as the traditional "men's" work of the time, such as furniture building, woodwork, and so on. Gorgeous quilts were made for the purpose of keeping one warm, but they are also unique and beautiful. I feel so blessed to have in my home many of the things that my great-grandmother and grandmother made, including worn and loved quilts, delicate doll clothes, and embroidered linens. They are among my favorite things in the world. They represent to me not only my family's history, but also the history of creative work and expression and a simpler, slower way of family living.

Today we're blessed by many modern conveniences, and I don't suggest that we give those up (though perhaps we could do without some of them). I'm also not suggesting for a moment that we want to replicate life during the Depression. But I do think we could take a lesson from the people in our recent past and not only use less stuff but also be more thoughtful in the disposal of that stuff. By trying to live more thoughtfully, we encourage resourcefulness, creativity, and alternatives to the standard answer of "buy a new one" that hurts not only our planet, but also our hearts and creative spirits.

Many of our children don't have the blessing of knowing people from generations past or the benefit of hearing their stories from an earlier way of life. It's our job to relay these messages of a simpler time to our lives as a family and to share the goals and values of creativity and resourcefulness. The activities in this chapter are all based on the idea that "less is more" and that giving things and materials a second life as something else can be one of the most satisfying of creative expressions.

ALTERNATIVE ART MATERIALS

While it's important to have good-quality art materials around you, it's also important (and fun) to look around for alternative materials of the free, recycled, and edible (yes, edible!) variety. Here are some ideas on where to begin looking for such materials.

Bowls of grains and beans from our pantry are ready and waiting to be turned into art.

The Pantry

This makes for a perfect opportunity to clean out any food that might be too old to eat (but not necessarily too old to play with). Think beyond the pasta necklace, and head for other grains, beans, and seeds. Think about color and texture as you pick your materials. Your chosen food can become the contents of shakers, objects to be glued on paper or wood, or baubles to be strung.

Nature

There's no greater source for materials than out in the world. Look for small rocks, leaves, acorns, bark, pinecones, and more. The hunt for material will become an adventure itself. These items, along with a bit of glue and paper or wood, can become a beautiful collection of mixed media art by your little ones. To take it a step further, use natural glue for your collages.

Recipe for Natural Glue

Combine a 3:1 ratio of flour and sugar in a saucepan. Slowly add cold water until a paste forms. Stir over heat until the mixture thickens. Add 1 teaspoon of white vinegar. This glue will keep in the refrigerator for a few weeks. Allow the glue to warm to room temperature before using it.

Trash

Yes, you read that right. I mean the garbage—or perhaps a bit less frightening, the recycling bins. Take some inspiration from the great recycling artists out there and get creative with the stuff that you (or others) are getting rid of. We keep an art box for the kids full of random pieces that are otherwise headed for the trash: old newspapers for papier-mâché, magazines and old calendars for collages, old electronics to "make" new ones. With a free imagination, they can turn into just about anything.

Thrift Shop

Scour your local thrift or charity shop for alternative art materials at a good price. Dishes, fabrics, leather—so many "thrifted" things can have a new life when you and your children put your creative minds to the task.

CLOTHING RECONSTRUCTION

Don't throw away those old clothes yet! Remember the days of yore when every bit of clothing was saved and somehow reused as another piece of clothing or fabric for some other purpose. We're all doing our best to throw away a little bit less than we're used to, and clothing is a perfect place to start. Clothes unsuitable for wear or that you aren't planning to donate can easily be reworked into new clothing. There's an abundance of crafters out there doing just that—recycling clothes into new ones or "reconstructing" them. (Some books on this topic are listed in the Resource Guide, or you can do an online search using the keywords *clothing reconstruction*.) Not only does this save on the amount of trash we generate and the amount of clothing we demand to be produced, but it's also an amazingly creative way to express ourselves and our sense of individuality. What a gift to a child not only to have the skill to create their own clothing, but to have the confidence and creativity to wear something that is truly them and not just like the same shirt that thousands of other people are wearing. You'll be able to give your clothing as much character as the unique person wearing it.

Virtually any piece of clothing can be reconstructed somehow. Look through your discarded clothing—things that are too small, too big, that you never wear, or that are headed out to donation or the trash. Are there aspects of these clothes that you really like? The fabric? A color? A style? These are good pieces to start with. Once you've found a piece of clothing that you'd like to reconstruct, sewing it is the most obvious way to re-create it into something else, but if sewing isn't your thing, try one of the following ideas with (or for) your children.

Dyeing

Perhaps with a bit of color you'll see this item in a new light. This is particularly true for my sweet Ezra, who really *wears* his shirts until they are covered with a mix of mud, marker, and spaghetti sauce. Tossing a few of these in a bit of dye gives him a whole new wardrobe! Later on in this chapter, you'll find instructions for making natural dyes.

Embellishing

What can you do to that shirt that might make it more fun for you or your child? Does it need some buttons sewn on? Some stencils created for it (see chapter 5)? Perhaps some beads, a bit of trim, or a little extra fabric will turn it into something you love.

Sewing

Then there are the endless possibilities of what your clothing can become with the help of your sewing machine or just a needle and thread—putting pieces of clothing together, swapping sleeves with another shirt, and so much more. Look at magazines or online for ideas that inspire you. Your clothing can also be used for many things other than reconstructed clothing. What else can you do with it?

Beanbags

A fun toy can be made easily by saving old clothing, cutting it up into squares, and sewing them together. It can be filled with beans, rice, or another grain you have on hand. (See the Wool Felt Block in chapter 2.)

Smaller Clothes

I use shirts from my husband, Steve, and I to make clothes for our youngest family members. Cut just the right way, a large adult's shirt can provide enough fabric to make a pair of baby or child's pants or shorts. (See the following section for how to do this.)

Constructing Children's Pants

With a bit of sewing experience, you can easily turn old, unwanted adult clothing into clothes sized just right for the little ones in your life. The following instructions are for turning an adult's shirt into a pair of toddler's pants. A large men's shirt can make a pair of pants for a child up to about age three or shorts for a child under ten.

What You'll Need

- One adult's shirt, from your closet or the thrift store (Flannel, knit, or cotton all work well for this project. Keep in mind that knit jersey will stretch quite a bit as you sew.)
- A pair of elastic-waisted pants or shorts that are the appropriate size for your child (These will be used only for tracing the size.)
- Waistband elastic, $^3/_4$-inch width. (Length should be your child's waist measurement plus 1 inch.)
- Needle, scissors, thread

A pair of pants, pinned onto the shirt, provides a size template for your pattern.

What to Do

1. Lay the shirt out flat. On top of it, place the pants to be traced, folded in half, with the outside leg of the pant along the side seam of the shirt. Place the hem of the pants along the hem of the shirt (this will save you from hemming the pants). Pin in place.
2. Cut around the pants, allowing ½ inch extra for seam allowance. At the top (the waist), leave an extra 2 ½ inches for the waistband (see photo).
3. Repeat this process on the other side of the shirt. At this point, you can trace the piece you just cut, rather than using the pants as a guide. This will ensure that the pieces are exactly the same size.
4. Open out the two pieces, and place them with right sides together. Pin in place. Sew from the top (waist) to the crotch, on both sides.
5. Open up the pants so that the crotch seam you just sewed is now in the center, and the two "legs" are on each side. Pin the pant legs together, matching up crotch seams and bottom hems.
6. Beginning at one hem, sew up the length of the pants to the crotch, and then down the other leg to the hem.
7. To make the waistband, fold down the top edge of the pants ¼ inch and press. Fold down another

1 inch and press again. Sew this down, close to the fold, all the way around the waistband of the pants, leaving a 2-inch opening at the back center to insert the elastic.

8. Using a large safety pin, insert the elastic through the opening and thread through, being careful not to twist. Sew the two ends of the elastic together where they meet.

9. Stitch the waistband to close the elastic opening. Turn pants right side out.

Your reconstructed pants are ready to go!

A "new" pair of pants for Adelaide, from Papa's "old" shirt.

Color from the Earth

Did you know that some of the richest dye colors might be right in your backyard? Dyeing with plants and other natural fibers can be fun and educational, as well as safe, inexpensive, and easy to do yourself, as well as with your children. This was the first method by which color was added to textiles and one that people have continued to return to as a way to connect to the earth and the colors it offers us. Dyeing with natural materials is something that requires experimentation—which is half the fun of this kind of project, especially with children. Depending on the season, the material you choose for a color, and the textile to be dyed, the variations are as many as the colors of the earth. Here are some suggestions to get you started:

Brown—oak bark, sumac leaves, coffee grounds, ground acorns, marigold

Orange/yellow—onion skins, turmeric, goldenrod

Pink/red—strawberries, roses, dandelion root, red leaves, beets, hibiscus

Blue/purple—iris roots, red cabbage, blueberries, blackberries, grapes

Green—grass, nettles, spinach leaves, lily of the valley, rhododendron

Following you will find some basic instructions for dyeing with natural materials, and the Resource Guide provides more to get you going in this area of creative play. This project does involve boiling hot water on a stove, which should be done only by an adult. Children can be involved in the process of selecting the materials and fabrics and, with supervision, in the dyeing process.

What You'll Need

- Salt
- Cold water
- Vinegar
- Large pot for boiling the plant material (You may want to use one that is not for cooking, as the process can stain the pot.)
- Rubber gloves, if desired (The dye color may stain your hands.)
- Fabric to dye (Muslin, silk, and cotton all work well. Start with a light color or white to get the best results and most vibrant colors. Fabric should be clean and dry when beginning.)
- Plant material (This will vary, depending on your location and the season. Remember never to take more from the plant than you need. Berries should be ripe and nuts and plants mature when selecting for dye. Do a search online for "natural dyes from plants" to get a complete list of plants to use for dye.)

What to Do

1. You will need to "set" the fabric in a fixative before beginning to dye. This will help prevent the color from washing out or fading. If you are using a plant to dye, you will need four parts water to one part vinegar. If you are using a berry to dye, you will use ½ cup salt to 8 cups cold water. Add your fabric to whichever mixture is suitable, and let simmer for at least an hour. Remove from the hot water, and rinse the fabric in cold water until it runs clear.

2. To make the dye bath, place your plant material in a large pot, and cover with water (you can experiment with how much water you want for different shades). Bring to a boil, and let simmer for an hour.

3. Strain the plant material from your water. Add your fabric to the drained water/dye.

4. Allow the fabric to soak as long as you like, anywhere from a couple of hours to overnight for a very strong color. The color will dry much lighter than it appears when wet.

5. You will want to wash your dyed fabric separately in cold water for the first few washings to see how the color holds up and to ensure that it doesn't bleed on your other laundry.

TOYS FROM NATURAL MATERIALS

We all know the cliché of a child who loves the wrapping paper more than the gift inside or the love that *every* child seems to have for a big cardboard box. In our cultural habit of buying what we want, sometimes the most perfect, simple "toys" are from materials that we overlook: those from the earth, those found in your home, those meant to be recycled, and those that may be free. Remind yourself to look around at what is available to you to find playthings, and your children will follow and find an endless supply of affordable, resourceful, and creative fun around them. Here are a few ideas to get you started.

Wood Blocks

The classic, perfect childhood toy—wooden blocks. But what about "imperfect" and true wooden blocks? Found, reclaimed, or fallen sticks and small logs can also make fun building materials for children. The wooden materials you play with don't have to be perfectly symmetrical or flat in order to create interesting or challenging projects. The more ambitious parent or one with good woodworking skills can cut found materials into small round disks using a handsaw or skill saw. With several sizes of logs, you can soon have an array of shapes and circles for stacking, building, and rolling. Go ahead and leave that beautiful bark right on there. If you'd like a smoother surface, use a fine sandpaper to even out the rough, sawed edges. These blocks offer a clear reminder of the trees from which they came.

Fabric Basket

Toddlers, especially, will love using fabric as a plaything because it will appeal to their developing tactile senses. I keep a small basket and put scraps of fabric in there, trying to cover a wide array of textures such as wools, cottons, and silks. Small children will use these for any number of things—from a game of peekaboo to a blanket for their doll, or simply for touching, rubbing, feeling, and sinking their hands into.

Yarn and String

A friend of ours once brought several skeins of natural fibered yarn to our playgroup of eight young toddlers. When we placed the balled yarn in the center of the circle of children, it quickly became the most desired, fun, and exciting plaything in the room. The balls were rolled, thrown, tossed about, and finally, unwound, wrapped, and touched. You wouldn't want to do this without an adult present, as the long strings could obviously be a danger. But with supervision, it's a wonderful sensory experience for young ones to touch, feel, and play with the natural fibers in yarn.

I like to be sure that my older children, perhaps by age four or five, have access to their own rolls and bits of string (along with tape, scissors, rulers, and glue). I've been amazed at the number of times and the number of ways in which this rope and string is used—hanging things from the ceiling, making marionettes, hanging clotheslines for their own clothes, and much more. In addition, my children have quite naturally learned several knots that I never knew or could have taught them, simply by trying things out and finding what worked for whatever they were up to.

Rocks, Shells, Acorns, and Pinecones

Yes, these are toys too. Look around you at the naturally occurring "gifts of the earth" and see their potential as toys. In our house, you'll find a basket full of rocks, one full of pinecones, and yet another full of shells. These aren't decorative objects (though I think they certainly are beautiful), but play materials. Rocks are used for stacking, cooking (Have you ever had the pleasure of dining on stone soup?), and designing beautiful arrangements. Pinecones become a challenging game of stacking. Acorns can become little dolls, and shells are often used as their home or bed. Again, keep in mind that with very small children you need to be cautious of choking hazards by keeping your natural playthings to a larger size. But once a child is past that age, a basket full of tiny shells and rocks can be a fun toy and feel *so* good to stick your hand into.

These are just a few ideas to get you started thinking about what might be around that your child and you might like to play with. The earth's gifts to us are plentiful, and our children will be blessed to know, hold, and play with those gifts.

part two

Playing

4

Encouraging Imagination

Imagination is more important that knowledge. For knowledge is limited to all we now know and understand, while imagination embraces the entire world, and all there ever will be to know and understand.

—Albert Einstein

Living a creative life is all about using our imagination. Like so many other things, imagination is hardly something we need to "give" our children, for it is simply a part of who they are. However, we do need not only to support and encourage the growth, stretching, and development of their imaginations, but to model the use of our own. While building a castle out of blocks or reading a story from a book comes rather easily to most adults, the imaginative play is often challenging for us to connect with. It is more difficult for our adult minds to dive into the latest character role that our little ones might assign us. But that challenge is certainly one we can rise to—and with great benefit to all. Once we do find ourselves in the midst of imaginative play with our children, we find that all the worries and cares of our adult minds are replaced by fun. Surely this is a skill that we could all improve on. Imaginative living needn't and shouldn't be limited to childhood, and it is our job to tell our children through our actions that their imaginations are something they can use, rely on, and find comfort in throughout their lives. It is through their strong sense of imagination that they will find solutions to life's puzzles and problems, create art in all its forms, and comfort themselves and those around them.

The activities in this chapter are all about imagination in childhood. They are about the ways in which we can encourage the skills of storytelling and imaginative play that can last a lifetime, as well as ways we can find to join in the fun.

WEAVING A STORY

Dunk is a friend of ours who lives alone in a house without his parents. He drives a big red pickup truck, and his little dog named Dot (a black dog with black spots) rides in the back. Earlier this year, we had a grand birthday party for Dunk's fourth birthday. A week later, we celebrated his third birthday. Dunk prefers chocolate, but in a pinch, he'll happily eat all of Ezra's broccoli.

Jo Jo Spirit loves clowns. In fact, sometimes Jo Jo Spirit is a clown himself. He can switch back and forth between being a clown and being a "regular" person with just the flip of a switch on his back—which is a trait we'd all like to have, isn't it? Jo Jo Spirit likes to play with blocks, a kind that you or I can't see or feel. His magic ability is that he can touch a lightbulb without getting burned.

Yes, Dunk and Jo Jo Spirit are both "special" friends to my children. Or as some might say, they are their imaginary friends. Each character appeared somewhere around the time Calvin and Ezra were each two and stayed with us for a few years, sometimes having more of a presence than other times. It astonishes me that imaginary friends used to be a source of concern to parents and medical professionals alike and were thought to represent immature thinking. Thankfully, the cultural perception of imaginary friends has changed in recent years, as most parents and professionals now recognize them for the benefits they provide children. It's now accepted that children can use imaginary friends to work out relationship issues, to work on conflict resolution, and to practice friendships. Not only can imaginary friends offer entertainment and companionship for children, but by nature, they also act as great exercises in creative expression. Frankly, each time that an imaginary friend has appeared in our home, I've been thrilled by their appearance as a sign of a healthy, thriving imagination and creative mind. To break it down to the truth of the matter, it's fun to have these special guests.

I encourage you to think about imaginary friends as a form of creative play and expression. If you should be so lucky as to have one appear in your family, I encourage you to let your child lead the plot of the story, and honor, welcome, and play with it yourself. Sometimes that means setting an extra place at the table for our friend; buckling them into the car seat; or in a moment of boredom, inviting the play by asking, "Shall we play Dunk and Dot?" just as we would ask, "Would you like to paint?"

Imaginary friend play is just one example of a way to create stories. Playing with dolls, puppets, and other toys are equally excellent opportunities for honing your creative storytelling skills as a family. Let your young children play with the lines of reality and imagination to figure out what the line is themselves, and explore the reaches of their young, developing, creative minds. Oh, the stories they'll tell!

Calvin and Ezra celebrate one of Dunk's many fourth birthdays.

THE POWER OF IMAGINATIVE PLAY

The real magic wand is the child's own mind.
—Jose Ortega y Gasset

Ah, the power and beauty of dress up. Dress up, and the creative play that ensues once the costumes are on, is the favorite form of creative expression in our home. From morning to night, our children act out their favorite characters from books, performances, their lives, and their imaginations. At any given time, we might walk around the corner to find a gymnast walking on a tightrope, a pirate digging for buried treasure, or Dorothy walking along the Yellow Brick Road with her friends. Our little ones wake up in the morning and dress immediately in their chosen costumes for the day; by evening, they have changed their costumes more times than we can count (or pick up, for that matter). Through this primary play in our family life, we have learned history, arithmetic, mythology, and science by exploring the lives and worlds of our characters together. Additionally, we've gained tremendous knowledge of design, art, and crafting in the construction of our costumes, sets, and props. Dress up has evolved into a natural foundation of our family's home education, play, and entertainment all rolled into one.

I'll admit that perhaps our family's emphasis on dress up might be a bit on the extreme side. I do wish, however, that every child could have access to at least a small box or trunk full of dress-up clothes— with a mirror beside it. I believe that watching themselves transform gives them the knowledge and power to recognize that they can create change in their lives. They learn and know that with the simple act of adding a hat, a shawl, or a fake moustache, they can be absolutely anything they want to be. Their imaginations open wide as their bodies become a blank canvas on which miracles can be created. Dress up can play an important role in growing up, learning, and developing our creative selves. Through dress up, our imagination comes alive and is asked to lead us wherever it likes. Ideas of gender, age, and even species are erased as a child stretches his or her ideas of self, life, and art, and gains a powerful ability to create on a three-dimensional, living canvas.

Dress up doesn't need to be extravagant, expensive, or messy. With the exception of a few gifts from generous and loving aunts, my children's dress-up collection has come entirely from thrift shops, our closets, and best of all, their grandparents' attics. Don't forget the advice from "The Best Toys" in chapter 2 when selecting dress-up clothes. Find clothing that will give the imagination room to breathe and come alive. If you're wondering what to include in your child's dress-up trunk, here are a few ideas to get you started:

- *Scarves*—A variety of colors can be transformed into skirts, headwear, dresses, capes, and much more.
- *Hats*—Vintage hats, in particular, have great appeal in their uniqueness.
- *Shoes*—Of course! Colorful, sparkly, and fun. (Don't worry about the orthopedics of these shoes, they're just for play!)
- *Accessories*—In our home, these are key. Jewelry, goggles, ties, tights, glasses, and kneepads are my children's accessories of choice.
- *Makeup*—Face paint and makeup can be a lot of fun in dress up, but also messy. Save it for "special" performance days or a rainy day if having it accessible all the time isn't practical for your family.

Of course, there is often concern over the storage of all of these props. Clothes and accessories can quickly pile up and clutter the house. Since this has been an issue we've struggled with in our home in past years, let me share with you a few tips that have helped us manage the dress-up clothing pile monster.

- *Racks*—On hangers is the best way to see all the clothes, but not the easiest for children to care for themselves. It's a great solution for older children who are able to reach and use hangers or parents who don't mind the daily chore of hanging up.

- *Pegs*—If space is available, a row (or rows) of pegs can be a way to store the clothing so it's easy for children to find and care for themselves.
- *Suitcases*—My favorite way to store dress-up clothes is in suitcases. They're easy for children to fill up and great for carting to the backyard circus tent or whatever stage you have. I also particularly love the look of a stack of vintage suitcases.
- *Trunks and baskets*—A large trunk makes for supereasy cleanup. Add a few small baskets for the smaller items so they don't get lost in the jumble, and this may be the best solution for both children and parents.

Calvin begins the transformation into another character with a bit of face paint.

ON STAGE

> Ladies and gentlemen, please take your seats!
> The performance is about to begin!
>
> —Ezra Stanley Soule

So you've got a pile of imaginative dress-up clothes accumulated and an eager child (and, admit it, an eager parent too). What's next? Sometimes it's the act of dressing up and then dressing up again (and again) that is the activity itself. Other times, and for many children, it's the creation of something more once the dress up has happened. It's showtime, my friends. And wow, are you in for a treat.

A home stage can truly be set up anywhere: the carpet, deck, sunporch, or coffee table (often the favorite "stage" for my children). It can be a real treat to create a home play theater for your family. The following are a few different ways in which you can make a space for the theatrics to happen.

Doorway Theater

Deep in a Maine winter, with a strong love of *The Wizard of Oz* happening all around us, we had the idea to make a doorway theater curtain in the double-door-sized opening between our dining and living rooms. I bought a shower curtain tension rod and used two long curtain panels. As simple as that, we instantly had a stage, a backstage (the dining room, which quickly filled up with props), and supercomfortable chairs for the audience (if only we could take the couch to *all* performances). After adding a few flashlights for the spotlights, we might as well have been on Broadway. This theater stayed up for months and saw use every day as one performance after another was practiced, dress rehearsed, and ultimately "performed." When I needed the doorway free and it wasn't being used by the children, I just pushed the curtain panels to the side as you would on a window, so that they were out of the way. The tension rod is easy to take down and put back up quickly, so the curtains and rod can be stored in a closet or somewhere out of the way until showtime.

A smaller tension rod can be used on a smaller doorway and is particularly good for a puppet show theater. Tension rods and smaller curtains will fit perfectly in a standard-size door opening. Hang the rod low enough so that the curtain reaches the floor, place a stool behind it, hand your little one (or yourself) a few puppets, and you're in for a perfect puppet show!

Our backyard playset becomes an impromptu circus tent.

Clothesline Theater

Perfect for an outdoor performance in the summer (perhaps a circus or a concert in the park?), a clothesline theater is another great way to keep the theatrics alive at your house. Use clothesline to hang an old sheet as a backdrop, which can be painted with acrylic paints and hung with sturdy clothespins or binder clips. For the front "curtains," hang another rope length parallel to the first and use either curtain panels (the opening will make it easier for the children to slide it themselves), sheets, or fabric.

PLAYING IN THE PARLOR

It's probably hard for any of us, much less our children, to imagine a time before computers and television or even radio, when families gathered after an evening meal for some entertainment and play with each other rather than with electronics. Traditional parlor games, those that do not require any materials, such as a board or cards, are one of the ways families passed the time together. These games provided a way for them to be together—imagining, creating, and playing. Blindman's buff and charades are perhaps the games that have carried over most into our modern times, but there are many more that are similarly creative, open-ended, and fun for the whole family.

There seems to be less time in our lives for such games now, but I think that might be because we are out of the practice of playing together. So often, we separate to our own bedrooms or to playing with those our own age. I encourage you to give an evening of parlor games a try in your home after dinner some evening or on a regular night each week. The following are a few traditional Victorian parlor games that we've adapted and tweaked to suit our family. They can be adapted and played anywhere and by anyone, making them a great way for your family members to spend some time connecting with each other.

Whatever You Do, Don't Smile!

A big favorite in the two-to-four-year-old crowd, we've adapted the traditional Victorian game of If You Love Me Dearest, Smile. Everyone gathers in one room, and the person who is "it" walks from person to person saying, "Whatever you do, don't smile!" to which the recipient replies, "Whatever I do, I won't smile!" without a smile. The "it" person then moves on to the next person until they get a smile from someone, who then becomes the "it" person. The children have a fabulous time going from person to person, making silly faces, gestures, and voices, trying to get the family to laugh, which we always do.

A Twist on Charades

We like to play charades with a bit of a difference. First we choose a category, such as animals, emotions, or adverbs, and we write down several words related to that category on small pieces of paper. We put the pieces in a jar and then select something out of the jar to act out. Our family favorite is surely "emotions," which is not only fun, but also a healthy way to think about and act out feelings surrounded by the safety and support of those who love and care about us.

The Endless Story

I remember playing this game with my grandparents, and you might too—whether with your own grandparents or at summer camp. One person starts a story—it can be any story with any characters. That person tells the story for a given period of time (with our young children, we use a one-minute hourglass, which seems just about right). When the time is up, the storyteller stops, midsentence or not, and the next player takes over. The story takes twists and turns, and new characters emerge. This is a fun way for the whole family to create and imagine together.

What's in the Bag?

As another kind of twist on charades, we keep a bag of props that we pull out for this game. It's full of random bits and objects, such as kitchen items, fabrics, tools, anything you can imagine. Depending on how you'd like to play, one or two players choose an object and have thirty seconds to come up with a short skit based on the object they have. A wonderful improvisational performance ensues, entertaining us all.

5

Every child is an artist. The
problem is how to remain an
artist once we grow up.

—Pablo Picasso

Supporting Your Young Artist

I couldn't agree with that quote more. Everyone really is an artist, and the purest and truest artists among us are the very young. As they get older, they receive far too many messages about what art is and how to "do" art, so that before they know it they're adults who say, "I can't draw," and "I'm not an artist." Not true! We are all artists; it's just a matter of getting all that other stuff out of the way, all the things that we think art should look like.

As parents, we're given a tremendous opportunity to nurture, support, and encourage children in their early artistic expressions. A beautiful side effect of that effort is that we can nurture, support, and encourage our own artistic expression at the same time, even if we were never supported that way as children. Encouraging your young children can give them the confidence to carry them through, so that as adults they can say, "I am an artist," whether or not it becomes their passion or life focus. How true that is for all of us, and how wonderful it would be if we all could believe and accept that, for art has tremendous power—the power to express, the power to heal, the power to speak, and the power to connect people.

Watching three children develop their artistic selves has been a tremendous gift that I never imagined could be so amazing. I knew that I would enjoy, love, and be inspired by my children once they started drawing and painting, but I had no idea of the ways in which that would happen. The ways that each of them, in their own manner, have naturally discovered and expressed themselves through art is a joy to see. The uniqueness amazes me—how each has his or her own preference of what to work with, and the way they work is so very different. All of this, when I can step back and look at it, tells me so much about who they are, how they learn, and what they think. What a gift that is.

The key to successful art with children is a matter of a few simple things, namely access, exposure, and encouragement. First, access to materials. High-quality art materials that are always at their fingertips and ready for them to use when the inspiration strikes them are essential. A children's drawing table or desk, cleared of all but a pile of blank paper and crayons or markers, is a welcome invitation for a session of drawing play.

The second important element in raising confident artists is exposure to art of all kinds. Visit your art museums and galleries, and just walk around and talk about what you and they see. Soon, they'll be able to identify the way a brush was used, or the medium in which a piece was made. Visit your library for art books to bring home and explore. Stretch your own ideas of what art is to think about textiles or street art or anything else that isn't in the realm of classical art.

Lastly, encouragement is where we come in as parents. With young children, it's a matter of giving them the room to discover art for themselves and perhaps drawing or painting alongside them, modeling the use of the materials. Other than that, at the youngest age, your artist does not need instruction and certainly should never be told how to draw. Once they are old enough—you will know when the time is right, or they may tell you—your encouragement may change from silent guide and partner to seeker, when you begin to seek out the classes or instruction that your child is interested in.

The activities in this chapter will give you some concrete ideas on supporting your young artist, ways to connect as a family through art, and ideas on what to do with all that fabulous art once it's been created.

FAMILY DRAWING TIME

During the winter months, in particular, when we spend days upon days inside together, we often try to do a daily Family Drawing Time. This is a bit different from the wild and crazy, messy, and free experience that we have during other art or craft projects. Family Drawing Time can be a quieter, more specific, and inward-thinking time for drawing. It's a way for you and your child to each be creating for yourselves, side by side. Modeling this type of creativity will show your children how to do it themselves—how to reflect on ideas, imagine, and transfer them to paper. Family Drawing Time is a great exploration of imagination. Even if drawing isn't your thing, try to stick with it. Just put pencil to paper and doodle; watch your child for inspiration. You might be surprised at what you can create.

If your children are a bit older, it might be fun to turn Family Drawing Time into a still-life exploration. Take a nature walk together and find an object to bring home. Place it in the middle of the table, and use that as the object for each person to draw during Family Drawing Time. Ask questions about how the drawings are different, how each person saw the object, or the different drawing effects used. You don't need to know technical art terms to make this happen; just talk about what you see and what feelings it evokes. What a boost to your children's self-esteem this activity can be— giving them the language and confidence to say what they see in the art around them. Here are some tips to get you started on your own Family Drawing Time.

Be Prepared

It's helpful to set up everything on a table before you begin. With little children, I make sure that everyone is well fed and otherwise prepared to sit for a while. Eliminate as many distractions as you can (turn off the phone, music, and so on).

Use Special Drawing Books

Keep a special notebook for each person just for Family Drawing Time. This is different from the regular notebooks or paper that we use at other times. Children find it special to have something just for this occasion, and I think many adults would agree. Drawing books, journals—they're just fun, aren't they? After a time, when the book is filled, it's a wonderful confidence builder for your young artists to see just how much they have created and to see the evolution of their ideas and creativity as they've grown. The same applies to adults too! We're still learning, and our drawings will change to reflect that.

Gather Inspiration

Sometimes we all need a little nudge for inspiration when we get stuck. In the middle of the table, place some books for perusing. Books, magazine clippings, and photographs work well. Our favorite inspiration books are nature field guides—illustrations of trees, flowers, or insects—all beautiful things to look at and dream about transforming into art.

Limit the Conversation

This obviously varies, depending on the mood of the moment and the age of your children, but trying to keep a quiet, reflective mood really encourages contemplative drawing best. Experiment to find what works well for your family in this regard—perhaps some classical music would be helpful, or maybe just silence.

Work Together, But in Peace

This isn't necessarily a time for drawing together. If more cooperative, collaborative drawing and play is happening during the rest of the day and that need has already been met, you'll have a greater chance of Family Drawing Time working well. You'll be drawing alone but side by side, inspired by each other but working on your own projects. It's a way for parents to get a bit of quiet thinking and creating time and for children to witness that process in action, as well as experiencing it for themselves. It's a time for each person to be creating for himself or herself.

Use Cool Stuff

It really does make a difference to use good-quality art materials. The experience of drawing is enhanced so much by supplies that work. Family Drawing Time could be the time that you bring out the "good stuff" if it's not otherwise out for general use. (See "Use the Good Stuff" in chapter 2 for more ideas about the materials you choose.)

Be Flexible

Perhaps the most important tip of all: If Family Drawing Time isn't working at a certain moment, let it go. But don't give up and think it can't work for you; just try again later. The creativity will only flow when everyone is happy.

Family Drawing Time in progress.

ART-ON-THE-GO BAGS

We've already talked about keeping your home stocked and at the ready with art supplies for when childhood inspiration strikes, but what about when you're out? What about the nature walks, the parks, the city streets where every artist—even the young among us—finds tremendous inspiration? I've been making these Art-on-the-Go Bags as children's gifts for several years, and they've all been met with much love. These traveling art bags can be carried to those favorite inspiration spots and be a complete little art studio in themselves. I usually sew a drawstring backpack for my bags. Alternatively, you could make a basic drawstring version of the Bedtime Bags in chapter 9. There are also backpacks—particularly drawstring bags—that can be found rather inexpensively and then filled with all you need for your traveling art studio. You'll figure out what you and your children use most often, particularly on the go, but this is what I stock inside our backpacks:

- A blank drawing book (We love Moleskine brand, and they become our special art books that we each treasure dearly.)
- Colored pencils in a Felt Pencil Roll (see chapter 2)
- Pencil sharpener
- Markers
- Drawing pencils
- Pens
- Nature field guides (We like to carry a book or two on wildflowers, birds, or insects to see more about what we are spotting on our adventures.)

Once your art bag is complete, head on out into the world to be inspired and create! Carry your art bag with you as you travel or leave it in your car so it will always be nearby when you're out and about. A park, a beach, a city square, the mountains, and your backyard—really, just about anywhere you go—can be brimming with inspiration for the artist within you. Speaking of that, do be sure to make a bag for yourself too.

FREEZER-PAPER STENCILING

A technique called "freezer-paper stenciling" has been a huge hit around our home lately. Freezer paper, a paper with one waxy side (also called "butcher paper"), is readily and economically available in most large grocery stores across the country and can also be found at some craft supply stores. (If you cannot find it locally, try searching for "freezer paper sheets" online or at quilting shops.) From the little ones creating the images to be stenciled to Mama and Papa cutting out the stencil, the result of this activity could be a "new" wardrobe for everyone. There are plenty of resources online about how to do this and where to find the stencils, but I'll share with you the method that has worked best for us.

What You'll Need

- Sheets of freezer paper
- Fabric paint

- X-acto knife (for parents' use only!)
- Self-healing mat or cardboard
- Stencil paintbrush
- Image to stencil (see the following pages for samples)
- Pen
- Iron (again, for parents' use only)
- Curved manicure scissors for rounded images (helpful but not necessary)

The freezer paper stencil process—the shirt in the middle is drying, while the one on the right is complete.

What to Do

1. Choose a fabric. The freezer-paper stencil can be done on any fabric; however, fabric high in polyester fiber might be a bit more challenging than cottons. We've done a lot of tote bags, as well as lots of T-shirts—either new, thrifted, or old (with the stencils conveniently placed over the stains).

2. Choose an image. When looking for an image to stencil, think about the outline of the shape. Simple images with little detail, such as stars, flowers, and birds, are best. Some sources for stencils are Google image searches (use *stencil* and *silhouette* as keywords), clip art found on your computer or online, stencil books, photographs, drawings, fabric, vintage cutouts and silhouettes, online stencil websites, and your or your child's own art. Some images have been included to get you started (see illustrations A and B). Once you've selected your image, place the freezer paper over the image to be traced (shiny side down), and trace the outline with a pen. (If you're using the sample templates given here you can trace right from the book, or photocopy them to the size you like.)

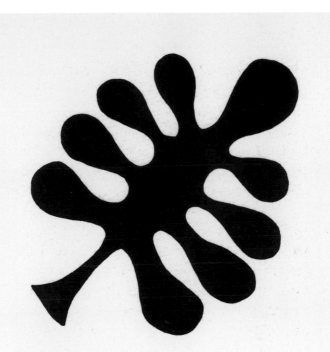

Illustration A.

3. Cut the stencil. This step will need to be done by an adult, as the knives can be very sharp. Place the freezer paper on cardboard, foam, or a self-healing mat (used for quilting), and cut the shape out with a craft utility knife (keeping the shiny side of the freezer paper down). A pair of curved manicure scissors works well for curved lines. Be sure your knife is sharp (the blade should be changed after every few stencils).

Illustration B.

4. Set up the stencil. Be sure that your fabric to be
    stenciled is clean and dry. Iron out any wrinkles.
    Place an extra piece of freezer paper (the same
    overall size as your stencil) under the fabric, shiny
    side up; this will help hold the stencil in place.
    Put the stencil, shiny side down, where you want
    it on the fabric. Iron lightly (twenty seconds at
    most) to "hold" the freezer paper in place.

5. Paint the stencil. Any fabric paint will work for this
    project, though I do prefer working with a higher-
    quality textile paint, which can be found at your

local craft supply store or online (see the Resource Guide). Using a paintbrush (I prefer stencil brushes, which control the paint coverage a bit), and following the manufacturer's directions, apply an even, single layer of paint to the inside of the cutout area of the stencil.

6. Once the paint has been applied, let it sit overnight. Do not remove the freezer paper, and try not to move the fabric. Once the stencil is dry (twelve hours or so), you can peel off the freezer paper. At this point, you may use a fine brush to add another layer or more detail to your piece, letting it sit again to dry, if necessary.

7. Set the stencil according to the directions on your paint. Usually, this involves ironing first the wrong side of the fabric and then the right side over the stencil for thirty seconds each on high heat. You can also heat set by tossing the stenciled fabric in the dryer for fifteen minutes. Be sure to follow the instructions on your fabric paint for the best results.

8. It's a good idea to wash your stenciled fabric by itself the first time. Depending on the fabric, the paint used, or the way it was set, it's possible to have some bleeding the first time it's washed. For best results, wash it alone in cold water. After that, it can be washed with other laundry.

DISPLAYING CHILDREN'S ART

How full is your refrigerator? No, the outside! Is it covered with your children's art? I love the way my little ones offer up their precious art for the prestigious position "on the fridge" and take such pride in it being placed there. If the artwork in your house is anything like the artwork in ours, in addition to a refrigerator full of art, there's a mountainous pile of pieces waiting their turn at being displayed or otherwise finding a home. Believing that it is so important for children's budding art expression to be supported and appreciated, we place much value and respect on their art, which means coming up with creative ways to display, showcase, and store all of it.

To control the day-to-day piles of paper that can accumulate, I keep an Art Box near our drawing space, where I keep drawings until their ultimate home can be decided. As we clean up our work and play spaces each day, I remove all the extras—all the pieces of art that got ripped, glued to bits beyond saving, or started but not finished. At our house, these pieces get cut up to use again as scrap paper or are recycled. Then, with all the other work that we want to save, I try to write quickly on the back in light pencil the name of the child, the date, and anything else I want to remember about the piece that isn't evident from looking at it (such as "Ezra says this is a picture of what he saw in his dream last night."). These pieces go right into our Art Box until they can find a home in one of the following places where our children's works of art live out the rest of their lives and where they can be revisited often. The following are some kid's art storage solutions that have worked in our home.

Art Boxes

I keep a box of "special treasures" for each child. This consists of a large box big enough for holding large pieces of artwork, cards, letters, notes, and other special mementos. Special artwork to keep for them until adulthood goes into these boxes, things I think they might like to have later on in their lives.

Art Books

This might work best for people who are inclined to record things in paper, such as scrapbookers. When Calvin was first beginning to draw, I bought a large, spiral-bound, blank book with the intention of putting samples and commentaries of his art in it. These books are not meant to be an exhaustive collection, just a sampling and a record of the evolution of the children's art that we keep in a read-ily available place, oftentimes as a coffee-table book. We all love por-ing through these books and looking back to see what the kids were drawing at certain ages. Often, with their older perspective, we hear reflections on what they were doing at the time. For example, when Calvin was five and we were looking at his drawings from age two, we found the very picture in which he first drew a body on a per-son, rather than the sweet hands and legs coming out of the head (oh, how adorable that is). As a five-year-old, he was able to tell us so much about that process, remembering drawing it and how it oc-curred to him that he was "forgetting the body." The art books, while personally challenging for me to keep up, have been a record that is well worth keeping for its memories and insight later on.

Beyond the storage need, it's also wonderful to display your children's artwork. Here are some display solutions that have worked in our home for making children's art more visible.

On the Walls

There is no art more beautiful to me than the art of a child. And what more wonderful testament to your love for it than by framing it and putting it up on your wall alongside the other "adult" art you may have purchased or created yourself. I try to frame a piece of my children's art every six months or so, and it gets added to our hallway of kids' art—a place where I believe anyone can find great inspiration. In addition to the wall specifically for art, there are pieces scattered throughout the house in various rooms, blending right in with the other art in our home. Whenever a new piece goes up, there's much excitement and commentary over it, as well as many lingering glances as the little one stops to reflect on his work.

A changing gallery of children's art evokes a sense of pride from the little artists.

Art Wire

A more temporary solution for display, an Art Wire is great for children to maintain themselves, switching the artwork that is most important to them at any given time on and off. An Art Wire is made quite simply with pushpins and light wire, string, or cord. Inserting the two pins into a wall, door, or cabinet, tie the string to each of them, creating a wire to hang and clip (clothespins work well) artwork to. We keep an Art Wire over our youngest's drawing table, so pieces can easily be viewed and added as Ezra sees fit. (See also the Inspiration Wire in chapter 1.)

Personalized Bulletin Board

A classic bulletin board is such an easy way to display kids' work and can be adapted easily to be visually more creative and personalized than the standard corkboard. Using a simple, store-bought piece of corkboard, cut a piece of fabric larger than your board, making sure you have 2 inches of extra fabric on all sides. Fold and staple the fabric to the back of the board, transforming your standard bulletin board into a personalized canvas for displaying your most precious art.

Art Clips

Like an Art Wire, Art Clips are an easy way for children to maintain the display of the artwork themselves. These clips can be hung permanently and strongly on the wall. The following are instructions for making your own Art Clips.

What You'll Need

- A wood board the size of your choosing (I suggest 1 × 3 inches.)
- Paint for the board
- Binder clips, found at any office supply store
- Wood screws

Easy-to-construct Art Clips are an accessible way for children to display their art.

What to Do

1. Paint the board any color you choose.
2. Using your wood screws, attach the binder clips to the board, screwing into the space at the top of the clip. Be sure to place them at appropriately spaced intervals, leaving enough room for a piece of paper to fit between them.
3. Attach the board to your wall space. If you'd like it to be accessible to your children, be sure the height is appropriate for them to reach.
4. Hang up those treasured pieces of art to look at.

CREATING WITH CHILDREN'S ART

Besides displaying, storing, and marveling at my children's art, my favorite thing to do with all that inspiration bursting out of them is to turn it into another creation. It's a joy to take a piece of their art, be inspired by it, and collaborate to then add my own ideas and creative expression. Here are a few of the ways we have done this in our home.

Embroidery

I love the lines and shapes of children's art, and embroidery feels like a wonderful way for me to, in effect, trace their work and really get into their heads about how and what their process is. I also love how simple it is to transform their two-dimensional art into a more textured version of itself that begs to be touched and loved. They are always so honored, pleased, and proud when their art makes its way onto my embroidery hoop, destined to become a pillow, wall hanging, or quilt. While the end result can be as complicated as you like, the initial act of taking a drawing and turning it into an embroidered piece is actually quite easy. There are a few different methods for doing this, but this is the one I use most often.

On a bright day, tape your child's artwork onto a window. Over this, tape a piece of fabric so that you can see the outline of the drawing through the fabric. I prefer working with linen for embroidery. Using a light pencil stroke (you can also use a wash-away fabric pen or pencil, found at your local craft store), trace the outline of the drawing onto the fabric. Taking everything off the window, place the fabric in your embroidery hoop, and begin. (See chapter 6 for more information on getting started on embroidery, or see the Resource Guide.)

Once the embroidery work is done, the possibilities are endless as to what to do with your finished piece. It can be framed as is or framed alongside the original drawing that inspired it. It can be turned into a pillow (see "A Visit from the Tooth Fairy" in chapter 10 for instructions on making a basic pillow shape), used as a patch on a piece of clothing, or incorporated into a larger project, such as a quilt or quilted wall hanging. When Calvin was four, I embroidered several of his animal drawings, along with his handwritten animal names, and used each as a square on a large quilt that was full of his drawings and my embroidered interpretations of them. This is now a favorite treasure of his—and mine as well.

Calvin's drawing is transformed into a pillow with some embroidery.

Fabric Transfers

Another favorite method of creating with my children's art involves the use of fabric printer paper. Adelaide's Birthday Book (in "Your Life Story" in chapter 8) is an example of this application. Pretreated and ready-to-print fabric printer sheets are available at your local craft store (look in the quilting section for printer fabric sheets). The fabric comes already adhered to standard-size copy paper, which can then be fed through your printer. Scanning a drawn image in and printing it onto the fabric provides a quick transfer of the image to fabric that can then be used as any other fabric—for clothing patches, pillow pieces, and quilting, just to name a few. The printer sheets have specific instructions on using them, as well as how to wash and care for the printed fabric.

Ezra's "moose with goggles" drawing is transferred to fabric and then embroidered.

Stuffed Art

In this project, a creation is drawn directly onto a piece of canvas, which is then sewn together, stuffed, and made into a three-dimensional object. Children are fascinated by watching their flat, two-dimensional drawing turned into a softie they can snuggle up with. This is a perfect project for a child who is beginning to sew by hand or as a collaborative project between the artist (child) and the sewer (adult).

Ezra's drawing of a "Chicken Cow" becomes three-dimensional when he stuffs and sews it.

What You'll Need

- Canvas or duck fabric in a light color, two pieces for each stuffed object, in a size of your choosing
- Embroidery floss in colors of your choosing

- Fabric pens, found at your local craft store (Be sure to use a permanent pen, not one that is intended to wash away.)
- Scissors
- Pins
- Embroidery needle
- Stuffing (I prefer working with natural materials such as wool or cotton—see Resource Guide—but any craft stuffing will do.)

What to Do

1. Using the fabric pens, you and your child can draw your "creature" on one piece of the fabric.
2. When the drawing has dried (usually almost instantly), cut the fabric following the creature's drawn outline, leaving about a ¾-inch space all the way around the edges.
3. Lay this piece of fabric over the second piece *wrong sides together*, pin in place, and trace the cut piece onto the second piece. Cut the second piece to match.
4. Now you or your child can begin sewing along the sides of the creature, in the ¾-inch space that was left along the edges. Keep the stitches fairly small to be sure the stuffing will stay in. Your stitches should be no more than ½ inch in length. Continue sewing all the way around the creature until

there is only a 2-inch opening, leaving the needle and thread still attached.

5. Stuff your creature with the stuffing you've chosen. Use only a few small bits at a time to prevent lumpiness, and continue stuffing until the creature is of desired firmness. (The stuffing process is always my children's favorite part!)

6. Once it is stuffed, continue the sewing where you left off, closing up the 2-inch opening.

7. Snuggle, show off, and love your new stuffed art.

Machine-Sewing Variation

If you'd prefer a seam for your edges rather than the exposed raw seams given above, you can also create your stuffed object on the sewing machine. From Step 3, place your fabric right sides together to cut the second piece. Pin in place. Sew with your sewing machine along the edges, and leave the opening as instructed in Step 4. Turn right side out and stuff. Close the 2-inch opening by hand sewing.

Embroidery Variation

This project can also be a fun way for children or adults to embroider. Using a wash-away fabric pen instead of a permanent one, create the drawing in the same way. Before cutting around the outline, though, place the fabric in an embroidery hoop and embroider along all the lines of the drawing. Continue following the remainder of the instructions.

6

Sharing the Tradition of Handmade

If we did the things we are capable of doing, we would literally astound ourselves.

—Thomas Edison

For whatever the political, social, or cultural reasons (and I think there are many), there has been a tremendous flood in recent years of people learning—or in some cases, relearning—and bringing the art of handwork into their lives. The age-old skills of knitting, crochet, embroidery, sewing, spinning, and more have seen a resurgence among people of all ages. I believe people crave a bit more of a simple, heartfelt, and handmade presence in their lives. They long for something unique and individual as an alternative to the manufactured. They are seeking a connection to their past in the way that handwork is a thread connecting generations. They are looking for ways to slow down and be more present, mindful, and full of intention in their busy, modern lives. And they want to share these ancient and rather sacred traditions of handwork with their children.

Children benefit from handwork for the same reasons that we do—from the resourcefulness, mindfulness, and the connection to our past—and perhaps even more. Young children learning the rhythm of using their hands for a craft will be creatively and intellectually stimulated by its presence in their lives. Their appreciation for the art of handmade objects will equal their confidence and excitement in their own ability to make things with their hands. The activities in this chapter will get you and your child started in handwork.

EMBROIDERING WITH CHILDREN

I think the best starting place for children learning handwork is with embroidery. Depending on the child and their interest level, the basic embroidery I'll describe can be done with someone as young as three years old. Like most activities at this age—or any age for that matter—the key is to set it up as an opportunity for success for your child (and yourself if this is your first time embroidering).

Beginning Embroidery

Easy-to-use burlap and a thick needle are a good place to start. Even if you're working with an older child, you still need to start at the beginning, and I believe this is a good beginning for anyone.

What You'll Need

- An embroidery hoop (For young children starting out, choose a large hoop, perhaps 6 inches in diameter or slightly larger.)
- A blunt sewing needle (In the embroidery section of your local craft store, you'll find tapestry needles that are a bit bigger than the standard hand-sewing needle and have a more rounded, blunt tip. This will work just fine with the beginning fabric you are going to use and be much safer for the little fingers holding it.)
- Burlap (If you don't have any burlap available—perhaps an empty bag of rice?—visit your local fabric store to purchase a yard. It's quite affordable and a bit scratchy, and it's just the right thickness for sending a blunt needle through to make embroidering easy with the youngest children.)
- Embroidery floss, found at any craft store, in a color (or colors) of your choosing
- Scissors

What to Do

1. Begin by cutting a square of your burlap slightly larger than the hoop with which you are working. Place this fabric in the embroidery hoop, securing the hoop so that the fabric is held taut. You will

likely need to repeat the tightening as you embroider, as it does loosen a bit with use and time.

2. Cut a strand of embroidery floss slightly longer than your child's arm's length (approximately 30 inches).

3. Thread the floss through the needle, and tie a small knot (you might need two knots to keep it from slipping through your fabric) at the loose end of the floss. Knots like this are not generally recommended for embroidery. Remember, though, that for a young child just beginning, the key is success and not perfection, so you needn't worry about the proper way to do things at this point.

4. You may also tie a simple slipknot with the thread around the eye of the needle, so that it doesn't slip out of the eye (again, not something you'd generally do with embroidery, but it's just fine for beginners).

5. The project is now ready to hand off to your child, who's eager to try their hand at stitching.

6. Instruct your child to start from behind the hoop and pull the needle up, then back down. Then from the bottom again. Again and again, they will soon find a rhythm, and perhaps just need gentle reminders once in a while that if the "floss is on the top, then you put the needle in through the top" and vice versa to avoid getting tangled.

7. When their floss is too short to continue, bring it
    to the back of the fabric and tie it off. If they're
    ready for more, then get them going! But if they'd
    rather stop for a break (it's hard work learning
    something new, isn't it?), encourage that too. I
    like to leave the burlap on the hoop for days at a
    time so they can pick it up as they feel moved to
    continue, much as I would on my own embroi-
    dery work.

*Ezra loves to embroider with
burlap and a safe blunt needle.*

It's best when children are starting out to plan on sitting alongside them to support and aid them as they need it. I find it sometimes helps to have an identical setup going myself so that I can model the way it is done, and they have a visual reminder to refer to when embroidering. The goal of this beginning embroidery is not to worry about stitches or design or any of that, but to get the feel (and love) of holding the hoop and needle in your hands. The pattern in which they sew matters little, and their stitches may actually be five inches in length—let them use the fabric as a blank canvas, drawing lines, shapes, letters, or whatever they prefer. My oldest child, Calvin, is quite detail-oriented and will only embroider when he can make it "look like something," whereas my more abstract-thinking Ezra is much more about the process and always surprised by the design that it creates. They all find their own way of doing things.

Intermediate Embroidery

Are you ready to move past the burlap and blunt needle to something more advanced? If you are, a more solid fabric can replace the burlap. I prefer working with 100 percent linen, but you can also use cotton, canvas, or broadcloth. You'll also need to leave the blunt needle behind and replace it with a needlepoint, embroidery, or tapestry needle (make a visit to the embroidery section of your local craft store). Designs for embroidery can be purchased and then ironed onto the fabric so you can embroider right on top of them. Making your own designs and transfers is fun and easy too. You can simply draw a design of your choosing lightly with a pencil or a fabric pen (the ink will wash out later). See chapter 5 for ideas on how to use your child's drawings for embroidery projects.

The split stitch (illustration A) and the backstitch (illustration B) are the two most basic and commonly used embroidery stitches. Many people spend their whole embroidery lives using just these one or two stitches—it really is that simple to get started. Depending on the thickness of the lines you are tracing and how thick you want the drawing to appear on your fabric, you might divide your embroidery floss into less than the standard six strands. I usually work with either three strands or six. Simply cut a length of the embroidery floss that you will use (24 inches is ample without getting in the way), and then divide the floss into whatever thickness you'd like.

If you're ready to move beyond these two stitches, then congratulations! See the handwork section of the Resource Guide for a list of resources on more ideas for embroidering with children and for yourself.

Illustration A.
The Split Stitch is used for
simple outlining.

Illustration B.
The Backstitch is used to create a
neat and clean line,
particularly in tight areas.

SEWING WITH CHILDREN

How many adults do you know who are able to do basic sewing and mending, such as sewing on a button, patching clothing, or stitching a tear? Surprisingly few of us have ever been taught the valuable life lessons of hand sewing and mending. This is quite a change from just a few decades ago, when this skill was necessary for everyone to know to some extent. Working on beginning sewing with your young children could very well be the start of a lifelong passion for creative sewing. Even if it doesn't become that for them, then at least it will surely be a valuable life skill that will encourage resourcefulness throughout their lives.

Like nearly everything we do as parents, I believe the best way to teach children sewing is to follow their lead and their interest in that direction. Surely an opportunity will come up that will relate to something they are interested in doing—making hand puppets, repairing some of their clothing, making something for a gift. The possibilities for introducing sewing are endless. The following are a few beginning activities, starting with one for the youngest sewers.

Handmade Sewing Cards

When a very young child is interested in sewing, sewing cards are a wonderful way to introduce the idea of a needle and how it works. The cards are available at toy stores, but why not make your own? They're the perfect sewing project for a young (three- or four-year-old) child.

What You'll Need

- Poster board, light cardboard, or cardstock-quality paper
- Permanent marker for drawing an image
- Scissors
- Paper hole punch
- Pieces of different colored yarn, cut into approximately 16-inch lengths with a knot on one end, or shoestrings
- Blunt-tip tapestry needle or transparent tape

Inexpensive and easy to make, these sewing cards are a great introduction to the concept of sewing for little ones.

What to Do

1. Draw an image on a piece of cardstock. You can also print an image from the computer and then glue it to the cardstock.
2. Cut a shape around the drawn image
3. Using the paper punch, make evenly spaced holes around the edges or outline of the image.
4. Tie the unknotted end of the yarn onto the blunt needle. If you would rather not use a needle, you can use a small piece of transparent tape to tie off one end of the yarn to taper it as a needle. Shoestrings also work well in place of the yarn.
5. Give your child the sewing card, and let them sew away! You can make several of them for variety.

Hand Sewing

In between Sewing Cards and the more advanced step of using a sewing machine is hand sewing. Several of the activities in this book are appropriate for a beginning hand-sewing project for children. The Stuffed Art activity (see chapter 5) is just right for the hand-sewing stage. Once you're tried that, the tooth pillow in "A Visit from the Tooth Fairy" (in chapter 10) is an excellent project as well.

A sewing basket for hand sewing makes a wonderful gift to put together for a child, so they can have all the materials and supplies they need readily at hand. In a beginning sewing kit, I would include the following:

- Thread in a variety of colors
- Hand-sewing needles
- Small scissors
- A thimble
- A ruler or tape measure
- A pincushion

Using a Sewing Machine

At some point, you and or your child might be interested and ready to move on to a sewing machine. If you don't already have one, sewing machines are readily available, and a good basic model is all you'll need. Sewing machines are also easy to come by at thrift shops and yard sales. When buying a used machine, look for a good brand name that you recognize, and to save yourself the frustration of trying to do this yourself, take it to a local sewing machine repair shop for a tune-up and evaluation. Ask around in your family about machines as well, because chances are, there's one right in a family member's attic that hasn't been used in years and is just waiting for a new generation of sewers to discover it.

Once you have a machine that is properly oiled and set up, a great way for young sewers to get familiar and comfortable with the machine is to use it without thread. Using an old needle and sewing with paper rather than fabric will give the young sewer a chance to learn the speed of the machine and how it operates without dealing with the frustration of tangled thread and fabric. Mark lines on the paper to try to trace with the needle, and practice turning, stopping, and backstitching. You can explore your machine freely this way, try out all the stitches, and generally get the feel for how it works and how you work with it.

A good basic guidebook to sewing is nice to have on hand. I've listed a few books in the Resource Guide that are geared toward both young children and adults learning to sew. But the traditional work of sewing has not changed that drastically in recent years, so an older thrifted or handed-down book on sewing will do just fine. You should have something that covers the basics of how to use a machine, how to use a pattern, the different supplies needed, and perhaps a few basic beginning patterns as well.

Choosing your first sewing machine project depends largely on age, ability, and interest. There are a number of projects in this book that are suitable for young sewers:

Felt Pencil Roll (chapter 2)

Wool Felt Block (chapter 2)

Stuffed Art (chapter 5)

Tooth Pillow (chapter 10)

I believe the main thing to think about when selecting a first project is making it fairly simple, giving the child (or adult) the quick sense of satisfaction and confidence they'll need to continue on to other, more advanced projects.

KNITTING WITH CHILDREN

Knitting has had such a presence in my family life that sometimes I wonder if my children will forever conjure up images of Mama with a ball of yarn and two (or more) knitting needles in her hands at all times. I always have at least one knitting project going on, and they're scattered throughout the house, along with the yarn, needles, and patterns that accompany them. The knitting is a part of our lives and a part of our home, as much as any of the children's toys.

Not to mention the results of all Mama's knitting time—all the socks, sweaters, and hats that have been made with love and intention and worn with pride and excitement.

As babies, my children would play with balls of wool and helped me unwind my purchased skeins into balls of yarn, singing this traditional rhyme to a tune I made up:

> Help me wind my ball of wool,
> Hold it gently, do not pull.
> Wind the wool and wind the wool,
> Around, around, around.

Right about the time each of them started talking, I remember that they asked for their own "knitting" (making Mama's heart double in size). Because they were a bit too young to really learn how to knit, I gave them each their very own knitting basket, just like mine. Their baskets consisted of a few bits from my own knitting supplies and materials—balls of yarn; large, blunt-tipped needles; measuring tape; and needle holders. All these little tools were played with over and over, alongside me, as they did their "knitting" too.

As they've grown, their interest has waxed and waned in wanting to learn to knit. Sometimes they're just as happy to play with the tools or take a turn with whatever project I might be working on, and sometimes they have really wanted to learn. We've started with finger knitting (sometimes also called "finger crochet") as early as four years old. When that has been mastered and they are ready for more, we bring out the needles and the real knitting begins.

There is an abundance of resources for teaching children how to knit, many of which I've included in the Resource Guide. But like most of the activities I've talked about in this book, I think the keys are patience and presence of mind when working with your child.

Start out giving your children their own knitting baskets for the early years, and then move on to finger knitting at ages four or five. If the interest and support is still present, they'll be ready for their first knitting with needles around age six. Try to steer your young knitters away from focusing on mistakes and instead help them to understand the beauty and character of those mistakes. The work of handmade is never perfect, and that's the beauty of it.

For me and so many others I know, knitting has an amazing power to slow life down in the best of ways. Its repetitive, rhythmic pattern feels meditative and makes me fully present in the moment. When I'm knitting, I feel more mindful, aware of what's going on around me, and connected to the people in my heart. Sharing this joy with my children feels like a tremendous gift to me.

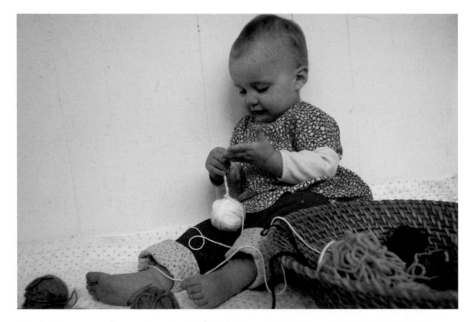

There's always a way for even the youngest of children to participate in most projects. Here, Adelaide explores and plays with balls of yarn "left over" from her brother's knitting lessons.

A Note on Materials

When first teaching (or learning) the craft of knitting, it might be tempting to use the inexpensive and more available materials such as aluminum knitting needles and acrylic yarn. I urge you to consider starting out with natural materials. Wooden knitting needles are readily available at your local yarn or craft store, or you can continue reading for instructions on making your own. Natural wool or cotton yarn is also easy to find, and the woolen variety is often available directly from the farmer who keeps the sheep—what a great lesson and gift for your children to know the source of their playthings. Keep in mind your children's innate connection to the earth and the natural materials it provides, and think of knitting as one more place where that connection can be strengthened by the materials you choose.

Finger Knitting

Finger knitting, as the name implies, is a method of knitting that requires only fingers as the "needles," and once figured out, can be a great way to introduce knitting to very young children. Instead of producing a piece of fabric, it creates a long chain. In the Waldorf Education tradition, finger knitting is introduced at approximately four years of age, when most children will be able to do it without assistance after being taught. You can find information, including photographic explanations, online or in some of the books listed in the Resource Guide. The basic instructions are as follows:

What to Do

1. Leaving a 6-inch tail, tie a slipknot on your index finger with the yarn. Let the tail fall down in front of your palm and slip the "ball" end of the yarn back over your index finger (see illustration C).
2. Pick up the knotted loop on your index finger with your other hand, pull it over the second loop and drop it off your index finger (see illustration D).
3. Repeat steps 1 and 2, gently pulling the ball end of the yarn taut each time (see illustration E).
4. Continue until the chain is the desired length. To finish, cut the yarn, leaving a few inches at the end. Finish your last loop and pull the end of the yarn tightly through this last loop to secure it.

Here's a rhyme that might help your little one learn finger knitting:

In the woods goes the hunter,
Round the tree goes the dog,
Out pops the rabbit,
And off they run!

Once your child has fallen in love with finger knitting (and I believe they will), there's a good chance that your home will soon be taken over by all the bits of chain they're making. If you're looking for some ideas for what to do with all that chain, try these:

- Ropes
- Belts
- Crowns
- String for making shapes
- Garland
- Doll hair

Or you can sew them together to create rugs, placemats, pot holders, and much more.

Illustration C.

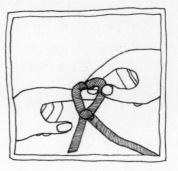

Illustration D.

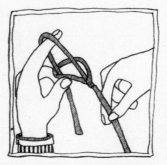

Illustration E.

Making Your Own Knitting Needles

Every resourceful, "knitterly" parent should know how to make their own knitting needles. This method is incredibly easy and very inexpensive. Did I mention that it's a lot of fun?

What You'll Need

- ¼-inch wooden dowels, found at your hardware or craft store (This will make approximately a U.S. size 10.5 needle set.)
- Sandpaper, both coarse and fine
- A pencil sharpener with various sized holes (The old, school-style sharpeners are best.)
- A handsaw
- Glue (Hot glue or superstrength glue is best.)
- Whatever decoration you'd like for the top of your knitting needles—acorn caps, clay balls, buttons, and so on (Keep in mind that you won't want it to be too heavy, or it could make knitting a bit awkward.)
- A finish for the needles, if desired (A food-grade mineral oil will make a natural finish for your needles.)
- Waxed paper

What to Do

1. Cut the dowels into 12-inch lengths.
2. Use the pencil sharpener to whittle one end of the dowel into a point. You don't want this to be

too sharp, or it will split your yarn. A blunt point is perfect.

3. Use the sandpaper—starting with coarse and moving to fine—to smooth the entire length of the dowel and prevent splinters.

4. Finish with a food-grade mineral oil, or leave the wood natural.

5. Glue your chosen end-cap decoration to the flat end of your needle.

6. Rub a piece of waxed paper over the length of your needles to give them a smooth surface for yarn to slide over.

7. You can experiment with different-sized dowels to make other sizes of knitting needles, but be sure that you have a pencil sharpener that's the appropriate size.

Inexpensive and unique knitting needles for all the knitters in the family.

FELTING WITH CHILDREN

Felting, also sometimes called "fulling," is the process by which raw, clean, and carded wool is agitated with warm, soapy water and forms into a hard shape as the fibers shrink and connect. This process can be done with loosely knitted items to give them a tighter, felted look and feel. You've probably done this by accident if you've ever shrunk a wool sweater in the wash. With raw wool, the process can be used to create pictures and objects. The Resource Guide has several books that will give you a more advanced look at what you can do with felt, for both children and adults.

I've included the basic instructions for making wool felt balls, a favorite activity at our house. The youngest children can be a part of this process, though you should have few expectations in terms of the results, particularly with small ones. Felting is a slow, tactile, and fun project; just a few felt balls will be created after a lot of work/play, so the emphasis should surely be on the process rather than the product.

What You'll Need

- Raw, carded wool (See the Resource Guide for where to find wool, but if you live in a farming area, visit your local sheep farm to see if they sell it. Wool can be purchased already dyed, or you can do so yourself with plant and natural dyes— see chapter 3.)

- Natural liquid dishwashing detergent
- Warm water
- Large bowl (One for each person works best.)
- Baking sheet or pan (one for each person)

Children love the process of felting and playing with soapy water and raw wool.

What to Do

1. Don that apron or smock; better yet, head to a table outside. This is going to be a wet one!

2. Fill your large bowls with very warm, soapy water. Use approximately 1 tablespoon of detergent for every 2 cups of water, and fill your bowls halfway. Place the bowls—one for each person felting—on the baking tray. This will help contain at least a bit of the dripping water.

3. Beginning with a small (child-sized) handful of wool, form it into a tight wad with your hands, wrapping it tightly with another layer of wool on top of it. Your ball, at this point, should be about the size of a large marble.

4. Keeping the ball as tight as you can, dip it into the soapy water, soak it thoroughly, and then remove it. Without squeezing, rapidly roll the ball back and forth in your hands with a bit of pressure. As the ball cools, dip it back into the water and begin rolling again. You want the water to remain fairly hot, so it will likely need to be changed during the process.

5. You can continue to add small layers of wool, dipping and rolling with each layer. Continue until the ball is the desired size and has become tight and a bit "harder" than the original loose wool.

6. Rinse gently with cool water. Place the ball on a dry, flat surface and let dry. This may take several days.

7. Once you have your felt balls, you can use them in so many ways: Several can be threaded together with a sharp needle to become a necklace or bracelet. They can be glued onto other projects as decorations. They can become juggling balls or the "eggs" for a play chicken. Strung together, they can also be a string of garland on your holiday tree. The possibilities are endless!

part three

Living

7

Exploring Through Nature

Flee to the Wilderness.
The one within, if you
can find it.

—Utah Philips

There's no greater source of creative inspiration, beauty, and art than the planet we live on. Nearly every artist will tell you that they draw great inspiration from the natural world—from the beauty in the falling leaves of a forest to the way a child's toes dig into the sand. As adults, many of our favorite childhood memories are connected with spots in nature—a walk in the woods behind Grandma's house, a neighborhood tree we climbed often, or a tree house we escaped to. Nature can be both our inspiration and our meditation. It can be a way that we connect with the earth and ourselves and, through that, find our creative spirits and energy.

I don't think there is anything more beautiful or inspiring to me than watching children just be in nature. When they are able to be free in their environment—free in mind and free in spirit—their inherent sense of connection to the earth is strong and alive. As a parent, I feel blessed and inspired to watch this process unfold throughout their childhoods.

It is important not only to spend time outdoors, but to bring the outside in as well. The things we surround ourselves with have a great impact on how we view our world. This is particularly true for our children, for whom everything is new and fresh. The beauty of the world around us—the changing color of the leaves on the trees, the smoothness of rocks at a beach, the acorns left behind in autumn—all of these objects are full of beauty and inspiration. Being around and in the natural world as much as possible should be a primary goal of childhood. But while that's not always possible (we all need to come inside and sleep most nights, don't we?), it is possible to bring a bit of the outside into our homes and, in effect, into our hearts and souls all the time.

The activities in this chapter are focused on our children and the creative ways in which they can and do connect with the natural world around them. I've also included ideas for incorporating the changing seasons within your home so that you can remember the outside world once you're inside.

FINDING YOUR SPOT

I believe it's important for everyone to have connections to a "spot"—or preferably, many—in our natural world: a special spot where you feel grounded in yourself and connected to the earth; a spot where you find peace and inspiration; a spot that brings you joy and peace in times of stress, sadness, and confusion; a spot you can conjure up mentally and emotionally, even when you're not actually there.

Don't let your financial or geographical circumstances get in the way of having a spot. You don't need to live in a remote rural area to have one; nature can be found in the middle of the woods, the middle of a city, or the middle of your home. And your spot needn't be an elaborate place; it can be anything from a house built in the treetops to a pot of basil standing in your kitchen. It doesn't matter what you choose for a spot; what matters is the connection you are making to the earth, the natural world, and ultimately yourselves.

You probably already have spots in your lives that you just haven't thought of as such, but I encourage you to do so. Start thinking of your spot as yours, and try to spend more time there. Close your eyes and try to hear, touch, and feel your spot so that you may know it as wholly as possible. Allow yourself to just be in your spot, both alone and as a family—I'm sure beautiful moments will be made. The following are some ideas of "spots" in nature that will hopefully inspire you to find or claim a spot of your own—one that speaks to you and your children.

- *A large rock on a forest path.* A rock that you come across often in your travels, that you can measure your children's growing height against, that you've spent time with, and that you know the feel of.
- *A child's garden.* A spot that is planned, designed, nurtured, and cared for primarily by your child. Where they will come to know the soil and what grows well in it. Where they can remember from year to year what was planted, where, how it grew, and especially what it tasted or looked like.
- *A climbing tree.* A tree that your child is able to climb higher and higher into each year. One that you study to find its species, size, and history; one on which you

know the missing branches. One that you watch change through the seasons, and see the wildlife living in or visiting. A tree at which you sit and think and feel.

- *A port city ferry terminal.* A spot where you witness the meeting of nature and human beings. Where you can watch the ways in which people connect, respond, and interact with the vast ocean in front of them. Where you know the type of birds that will appear and can sense their behavior and patterns of flight. Where you hear the sounds of the waves, the harbor activity, and the birds.

- *A flower box outside your window.* A spot where you can watch seedlings turn into flowering plants. A spot that in-sects may visit, and where you can watch the changing of a plant with sun and light, and know what it will look like under the evening sky.

- *A tree house.* A spot in the trees that you build and play in. A spot where you feel as though you are one of the birds, up in the trees, watching the world around, above, and below you.

- *A pot of basil grown in your home.* A plant you can nurture and watch and know when it is just right for eating,

- *A city park bench.* A spot where you can hear the mix of people, animals, and nature coming together. Where you see people interacting, animals living, and nature thriving with lots of life around it.

- *A lakeside dock.* A place where you hear the peaceful lap-ping of the water on the shore. Where you anticipate the call of a loon, the jump of a fish, the splash of a beaver's tail. A spot you see change from year to year due to more or less rainwater. A lake where your toes know the temperature before touching the water.

Feeling a connection to the earth and knowing a special spot in the world will nurture a deep love of nature in your children. It is only when we love the earth with passion and intent that we are able to care for, help, and heal it as well.

SEEKING THE WILD

It doesn't seem to matter whether it's a small patch of dandelions on a tiny strip of city grass or a remote, wide-open lake with room to explore. Whatever the size, whatever the landscape, children have an innate connection to their surroundings. It is when they are in these surroundings that they can find such beauty, enjoy such bliss, and create such imaginative and carefree play. I know I am not alone in having some of my fondest childhood memories revolve around playing outside, with my only toys being the ones the earth provided for me—building homes for the squirrels, running in and around the trees, building a forest of sticks and rocks, covering the ones I loved in sand. When I am

Ezra runs to the water, his favorite spot.

with my children out in the world, I see them experiencing the same things. I watch them weave their way around the trees in a forest; jump into the ocean with abandon; and wrap their hands around a pine tree as they climb, getting covered in sap and loving the sticky feeling on their fingers. They aren't worried about tripping on the roots above the ground, whether or not the water is too cold, whether they have dry clothes to change into, or how many days it will be before all the sap is washed off their hands. These details are the details of adults. It is the job of children to just be in the world. To know it and to fall in love with it. There are no rules in the wilderness; there are no right ways to do things and no limits on what their imaginations can dream up. It is this that makes the wild so critical to their creative growth: limitless freedom and imagination. Every child I have seen can certainly rise to the challenge of creating in the woods. They know how to do this; we just need to give them the space.

I would encourage you, if you don't already, to create a space in your family's life for time spent exploring the world around you, whether it is a weeklong backpacking hike in the deep woods or an afternoon trip to Central Park. Find what works best for your family and your interests, and make it a regular part of your lives. Not just the "annual" camping trip, but a regular part of your weekly and, if you can manage, even daily lives. Take advantage of the work of your local land trust and land conservation organizations to discover the woods right in your own backyard. Both urban and rural dwellers have many spots of wilderness to share. Let your children know them.

Questing

Our ancestors instinctively knew how to walk through the world— through a forest, through a desert, across a river—and "read" the signs around them. They did so in order to understand a new landscape, to find food, to remember their way home—they did so in order to survive. While the need for survival is certainly not the same today, it does seem that we instinctively want to continue searching, hunting, and seeking in the landscape around us. It's fun, it's imaginative, and it's an adventure. When we are actively seeking, we are fully alive. All of our senses peak as we take in the world around us, and we become present in and full of our surroundings.

Questing is an old tradition that is growing in popularity in the United States and throughout the world. It combines elements of nature exploration, creativity, treasure hunting, community building, and place-based education. Following treasure maps, clues, and hints left by a network of other seekers, you travel through nature to find a hidden object. Through this process, you learn not only the details of a place, but also the spirit of that place. The energy, the atmosphere, the connection to the earth are tangible and experiential things in questing. This is a wonderful opportunity for families to spend time together in their natural world, seeking and searching as a team. It provides not only a connection to the earth, but to a community of fellow seekers as well. More information about questing and how you can get started exploring can be found in the Resource Guide.

The possibilities for creative play are truly endless in nature.

GARDEN JOURNAL

> I have great faith in a seed. Convince me that
> you have a seed there, and I am prepared to ex-
> pect wonders.
>
> —Henry David Thoreau

Most adults who garden discovered their love of gardening as children. If the idea of a garden sounds overwhelming to you—with all of the soil preparation, the seed selection, the weeding and watering—then start small. A garden doesn't need to be elaborate and large to provide us with lessons and a chance for creative exploration. It doesn't even need to be outside. A windowsill pot of basil or a basic basement plant are both great, easy ways to fit gardening into your life.

If you already garden, give your child a small plot of his own to play with. Let him choose what to grow and decide how to grow it and care for it. If you have a young child, some assistance is helpful, but never force a child to garden. You will probably need to do a lot of behind-the-scenes maintenance to a young one's garden, so keep that in mind when determining the size, and try not to carry the expectation of them maintaining it if it's unrealistic for their age. With young children, eliminate the expectation of getting lots of "real" gardening done. Gardening with children should be about exploration, questions, discovery, natural learning, and play. Move piles of dirt around, pull some weeds, watch the bugs, and catch a toad. Marvel at the mysteries of nature and gardening with them. Show them how much you love it, and they will surely follow along and find their own love. As your children get older, they can take a lead in gardening themselves, with you there to assist, guide, and join in their fun. But when they are young, it's all about the play and fun of gardening. Plant vegetables they love and plants that you know will be successful and encouraging to a young gardener. Depending on your climate, sunflowers, zucchini, and pumpkins are all pretty much "sure things" that will bring smiles to your little ones' faces as they help and anticipate them growing.

Gardening is truly a creative activity, and the best gardeners plan, design, and record their work. Give your children the space to record their discoveries about the world through gardening with their very own Garden Journals. Begin by giving them a blank, unlined sketchbook with thick paper (for lots of different art mediums to work on), and designate it their Garden Journal. Make this special book just for the purpose of drawing nature and recording the garden. A Garden Journal can be a way to record the growth of your plants/garden from season to season and year to year. Here are some suggestions for what you can include in this book. Don't forget that these suggestions can just as easily be adapted to a pot of basil on your windowsill rather than a full vegetable garden. It's all gardening!

Draw a Garden Plan

Let your imagination run wild as you picture what your plant or garden might look like. How will you set it up? How will you mark the rows? How will you water the plants? For an indoor garden, what pots or containers will you use?

Design Plant Markers

Use the Garden Journal to design plant markers for your garden. Cut them out and laminate them (our preferred method is covering labels in clear packing tape). Then place them on a stick to mark the garden or plant.

What's in the Garden?

Draw the vegetables and plants you'd like to see. And don't forget the garden "creatures" too! A scarecrow and its visiting crows? What about all those crawly worms and bugs and snakes?

Draw Your Observations

This could fill a whole book. Make it easy for your children to take their journal and some colored pencils out into the garden to sit for a spell and draw what they see. The plants, the insects, and the food are all good fodder for a young, inspired artist.

Draw the Projected Growth

What fun it is to draw what you imagine and hope the garden will look like at the end of harvest time and then to compare it to reality when autumn arrives.

Record the Weather

This can be as simple as drawing a sun or a cloud for a young child. Soon, they'll see the correlation between a day of rain and a sudden growth in their sunflower stocks.

Garden Stories

That worm crawling through the zucchini plant? Surely he's on some kind of grand adventure that you and your little one can dream up. Use your garden to inspire fun and creative stories.

———

Your child's beautiful Garden Journal will document not only the growth of your garden, but also the growth of your child, who is perhaps a budding gardener himself.

The Garden Journal provides a wonderful opportunity for recording and remembering the small but important moments spent in the garden.

FAIRY HOUSES

One of my earliest memories is of being at my grandparents' camp on a lake in Maine and building a home for the squirrels. My memory of everything else about that trip is vague, but I recall fondly and clearly the feeling of working alone for what seemed like hours, busily stacking acorns for a gate, pine needles for soft beds, and twigs for the house. I went to bed dreaming of what would happen to the home and woke excitedly to see if the squirrels had moved in. A few twigs had moved in the night, and I was sure the squirrels had rested there. Perhaps they had.

Years later, my children have discovered a similar love in building fairy houses. I'm sure that children have always built "homes" like this in nature, but there seems to be a strong presence of fairy houses these days. Here in New England, at least, I believe this can be credited to Tracy Kane's book *Fairy Houses*, which tells the story of a little girl on vacation in Maine who finds a village of fairy houses and creates one herself. A dreamy and imaginative story, it has now been adapted into video and a live theater performance. In addition, more and more villages of fairy houses have cropped up throughout New England—spots where you'll find a gathering of fairy homes in the woods, tucked discreetly along a trail.

You needn't have a fairy village near you to make your first fairy house. With the fun nature of this activity, there's a likely chance that you will have a fairy village before you know it. The youngest (and oldest) family members can enjoy this activity, and you need nothing with you besides time, imagination, and the toys of the earth. Please keep in mind when building your fairy house to have as low of an impact on the environment as you can. Keep your materials natural, don't disturb living or growing plants, and keep your home natural-looking. This makes the fairies especially happy. This activity can be done in any landscape, as fairies really do go anywhere and everywhere on the beautiful earth—forest, riverside, desert, beach, and prairie fields.

In line with our local landscape, our fairy houses are often at the base of big tree trunks. There's no limit to how elaborate you can make your fairy's home—a house, beds, swings, gardens, furniture, hammocks, and so on. And all of this can be made from what you find around you: pine needles, pinecones, rocks, moss, shells, feathers, grass, acorn caps, sticks, leaves, and much more.

I think you'll be amazed at how much time you'll want to spend and how elaborate you'll want to make your fairy house. Just like when you were a child, this is an activity that is easy to get blissfully lost in. There's something special about making something so miniature and so magical as a house for the fairies. It's an activity that's a gift for you, your children, the earth, and those magical fairies too.

Calvin and I build a special home for the fairies.

CHANGING OF THE SEASONS

The decorating that takes place in our home is centered less on the traditional holidays that many people decorate for (such as Halloween, Christmas, or Easter) and more on the changes from season to season. This feels like a natural shift for us, and it seems normal that the decor and energy inside our home would change to match the changes outside. These changes are subtle but vibrant at the same time, and they're also a reflection of how we're spending our days. It may be a windowpane filled with leaves and waxed paper, a basket on our dining table full of shells gathered at the beach, a bedside table with a pile of pinecones next to the lamp, or a vase in each room filled with the dandelion picks of the day. It's something that we all do as we go about our days, gathering bits of what we love and bringing them into the inside space we share. Except for the intentional scattering that I do, for the most part, this decor is the result of the children's natural placement of things. A pocketful of acorns emptied onto their bathroom shelf at the end of a day seems more to me than just a mess—this little pile of acorns tells a story of how our time was spent and what my little one saw and valued as beautiful on our adventures.

Nature Table

Little bits of nature are scattered throughout the house for us to discover and reflect on, and they change often. However, there is one spot in our house that we use as a constant and consistent place for gathering these bits, and that is on our Nature Table. We began keeping a Nature Table when Calvin was just a young toddler. Some people like to keep similar tables as a display, but it was always important to us to make it something that was not only accessible, but also inviting for children to play with. For that reason, our Nature Table has changed greatly as our children have grown. In the beginning, we would keep it on a low shelf and keep large items on it for safety. As they got older and we didn't need to worry about chokeable items, we'd include smaller bits. Then when we had both younger and older children, we started keeping two tables—one with the big objects for the youngest and another, up a bit higher, for the older children who wanted to include smaller things. I keep a basket full of Nature Table materials in storage—play silks, water-color painting postcards, knit animals, felt gnomes, rocks, and shells. I clean out our table with each change of season, bringing the basket out and placing seasonal items on the table. But the table also changes from day to day as the children bring in their gathered bits of treasure. They spend thoughtful, reflective time moving things around on the table and creating scenes with the objects there. There are no rules about keeping a Nature Table, and yours can reflect whatever interests your family and whatever you have available for natural materials. To give you some ideas of what makes its way onto our Nature Table, here are some ideas based on the seasons.

Ezra adds little bits of found nature to our Autumnal Nature Table.

Spring

In the spring, our Nature Table is full of signs of new beginnings and reminders of the growth and renewal that is happening all around us. If you saw our table in the spring, you might find a budding leaf in a vase, moss, shells from our first beach trip, a watercolor post-card of tulips, driftwood, chicks and eggs, a found and abandoned bird's nest, a green play silk (see Resource Guide) to represent the grass, wheatgrass growing in a container, or springtime felt fairies.

Summer

This is the most plentiful time of year on our Nature Table, when you might find: shells, rocks, and sand from our beach visits; a blue play silk to represent the blue skies above us; picked flowers in tiny vases; frolicking felt gnomes and fairies; rocks from adventures in the woods; sticks; and driftwood.

Autumn

In the fall, our Nature Table is full of signs of the harvest with tiny gourds and pumpkins; felt pumpkins; a pile of fallen acorns; fallen wood; leaves of all colors; watercolors and paintings of the fall trees; and play silks in oranges, reds, and yellows to represent the changing colors outside.

Winter

The Nature Table is most bare and simplest in appearance in the winter season, as we use it to reflect the barrenness of what we see outside. For our New England landscape, this means white play silks to represent the snow on the ground; raw wool formed into snow friends; a single, small candle to remind us that the light will return; and perhaps red holly berries in a bowl.

Seasons Tree

One of my children's favorite pieces of natural home decorating is the Seasons Tree. I don't always have one out, but throughout the year at various seasonal celebrations, it makes its appearance. The Seasons Tree is something that sits in the center of our dining table and is a lovely mix of the outside world we love so much, as well as the inside handwork and crafting that we do. The basis of the Seasons Tree is as simple as a fallen and found tree, or rather a branch with lots of smaller branches on it. We place this branch in a glass, a vase, a jar, or a bowl filled with either dried beans, rocks, or shells, depending on the season and the weight of the branch. The filler will hold the branch in place in its bowl. Then the fun of decorating our Seasons Tree begins. Here are some of the ways we've used a Seasons Tree in our house.

Valentines

Fill the tree branches with heart ornaments. Use felt, paper, and lots of glue and embellishments to make hearts, and then place them on string or ribbon for hanging.

Springtime or Easter

The Seasons Tree is a perfect place to display your dyed, painted, and decorated eggs. Just glue a bit of ribbon, string, or fishing wire to the top of each egg, creating a loop for hanging on the branch.

May Day

For May Day and the celebration of spring, we decorate the tree in colorful pastels, with ribbons hanging from the branches (much the way a maypole looks), and if we're lucky, bits of the first tulips found outside as a garland intertwined with the branches.

Autumn

We don our bare tree with the colorful leaves of the fall season. With bits of paper, we draw or trace leaves, and then color or paint them in appropriate colors. We make a hole in the paper with a paper punch, and add string to hang. We've also made leaves from felt squares, hanging them with pieces of twine and string.

The Winter Solstice and Holidays

During the winter holidays, our Seasons Tree transforms into a small holiday tree of its own, covered with our handmade decorative crafts and ornaments. Another idea is to use the tree as an Advent calendar of sorts, with something hanging on the tree for each of the days leading up to your celebrated holiday.

8

If I had influence with the good fairy who is supposed to preside over the christening of all children, I should ask that her gift to each child in the world be a sense of wonder so indestructible that it would last throughout life.

—Rachel Carson

Capturing Moments

The one sentiment that I hear most often from other parents is how fleeting the time with their children really is. Particularly in the early years of parenting, it's easy to get bogged down by the details of the day-to-day and hour-to-hour care of young children, but experience tells us that this time is really short-lived, precious, and fleeting. Keeping this in mind, the activities in this chapter are full of ideas on ways we can creatively record, remember, and forever treasure this time we have with our children, as well as the ways we can share with our children how to creatively "capture the moments" of our lives together.

CHILDREN WITH CAMERAS

While I'm the one in the family who most often has the camera in my hands, I believe that Calvin is the best photographer (Adelaide and Ezra are still a wee bit young, but they'll join him soon). Children have such an amazing eye and see things very differently than we adults do. At the point in our lives that we become parents, we generally have many ideas of what a photograph *should* look like, *how* to take one, and *how* to edit them. Children, on the other hand, have the benefit of not knowing all the technical information associated with photography. They also have inherently fresh imaginations and great eyes. Not to mention, they've got a whole different height at which to see the world versus taller adult photographers!

Given the amount of technology associated with photography these days, there are a number of options that make it possible, easy, and affordable for children to be young photographers all on their own. Sharing a family camera is one solution, but if your camera is too precious to you (I'll admit that mine is), too difficult to use, or otherwise not accessible to your children, I encourage you to find a way for your children to have their own cameras. Here are some options to consider when choosing a camera for your child.

Film Camera

Point-and-shoot film cameras can be inexpensive and often sturdy enough to survive the bumps and jostles they may get from young children. The downsides are that the film development can get expensive, and once the film is gone, it's gone, so there's less room for experimenting with many photographs.

Digital Camera

The benefit of a digital camera is that your child can click away with no worries about running out of film. The downsides are fragility (though, increasingly, I see cameras made for children and built to withstand heavier use) and initial cost (but don't forget to compare this to film and development costs over the course of a year with a film camera). While some digital cameras out there are made specifically for children, be informed about the quality of the photographs they take. Taking pictures with a camera that takes poor photos is discouraging for anyone, let alone a child just starting out. Also keep in mind that unless your child is older, you will be the one editing, uploading, and printing the photos, so be prepared if this is the option you choose.

Polaroid Camera

Remember them? They're still around and actually have quite a large community of users who still love them. The cameras are very inexpensive to pick up used (on e-Bay, at yard sales or thrift stores), often for less than a dollar. And film for these cameras can easily be bought online. They're very easy to use, but again, once the film is gone, it's gone, and film for them can be costly.

We've tried a few different camera solutions with our children and right now are most happily in the land of Polaroid's One Step, 600-speed model, at least until they are a bit older, when a digital might be better and is less likely to be dropped as often as it would be now. There's something magical to children (and I remember this as a child too) about taking a picture and watching it transform before your eyes into a photograph. The instant gratification helps too, when we're talking about three- and five-year-olds.

There are many resources dedicated to teaching children photography, but when getting started, I believe they really just need basic instruction on how to use the camera they have. As they get older and their interest in photography increases, more instruction, classes, books, and workshops can be wonderful. In the meantime, encourage your children to take photographs of the world they see around them. They can take photos to keep, to display in your home, or to give as gifts to friends and family. The creations they can make with their photographs are endless—they can be incorporated into artwork or made into a book, newspaper, or game (a visual treasure hunt).

Once they start taking photographs, they'll surely need a special spot for storing them. Give them their own photo album just for their special photos, and it will quickly become something they are proud of. Give your children a camera, and encourage them to use them to use it however they wish to record the world around them and photograph what they see. I'm sure you'll learn something about them and their world by viewing their photographs!

Calvin captured this photo of his friend Ella working on her own photography (with her mama's camera).

SAVING SPACES

Do you ever wish you could go back to your childhood room and take a slow look around at, let's say, age five, seven, or fifteen? Do you wonder what was in that room, what it looked like after you left for school in the morning or before you went to bed at night? I think about this sometimes, even dreaming about the spaces I once lived in, wishing I could remember just what a room, house, or apartment looked like, places where I spent so much of my time and life. I'm often disappointed when I can't remember the details of a space I lived in or how I used it.

I hardly ever thought to photograph the nooks and crannies of a home until recently. In order to preserve in my mind some of my favorite spots and the flood of memories I treasure with them, I now try to take photographs of those spaces from time to time while we're still really living in them. These are the places in your home that bring you some sort of feeling of peace, joy, happiness, or comfort. A spot that reminds you of your children or one that reminds you of the way your family lives in it.

A favorite spot for Calvin, I photographed it for both him and me to remember later.

I encourage you to think about how you can save some of those space memories for you and your child. This time with your young ones is so fleeting; imagine how precious it will be to look at a photograph of a favorite play corner and let your imagination take you back. I'm not talking about chasing them around with a camera or documenting their whole lives in film (or digitally, as the case may be). But as you think of it, snap a shot of their bedrooms, their favorite play spots, and your family living space. Photograph spaces that are dear to your family. Some of my favorite spots are the little messes I find left behind at the end of the day, as these sights remind me of who my children are and what they are interested in at the moment: a pile of blocks with a beloved car as a "track," a doll tucked into "bed" on the couch at nighttime, or a messy desk brimming with projects and favorite things from the day. Encourage your children to do the same with their own photography, and see what spots in your home they consider special to them.

KEEPING IT ALL TOGETHER

If your family is anything like mine, and I'm guessing it is, then you too must be overloaded with the "stuff" of your children's lives. I'm talking about the stuff you want to save for them—the mementos, the cards, the artwork, the bits of their lives that you think they'll someday enjoy having themselves. You can't bear to part with those little daily treasures of art and craft and life, but let's face it—you can't store it all, either. In my six years of parenting, I think I tried virtually every method of saving and storing special things until I finally found these things that work best for my time, interest, and space.

And what about your children's special things, those things that matter to them most right now and that they treasure so dearly? Are their desks overflowing with notes from friends, drawings, ticket stubs, and dried leaves? With a bit of creative organizing, they can have their own special spots for such treasures too. Here are a few ideas that keep us creatively organized, inspired, and "preserved."

Children's Photo Albums

I love the idea of children having their own photo albums in addition to, and separate from, the family versions. These are photo albums that they can open again and again, pull the photos out if they want to, move them around, change them in and out—whatever they want to do because it is *their* album. This is not one where they have to worry about getting fingerprints on the photos or ruining the originals. Try to provide your children with their favorite photos, and when printing copies of your photos, order a few extras for their albums. If they're interested in organizing the pictures themselves, give them the freedom to do so. Empower them to organize and keep their memories the way they want to.

Treasure Boxes

A treasure box for every child, I say! Remember the real pirate-looking jewelry boxes from the seventies and eighties? I remember keeping my most treasured things in there, and it had such a special, magical feeling for me. My children have their own treasure boxes now. One has that big pirate box, and the other has a very special box he made out of cardboard, with glued bits and bobs of nature. Both boxes are full of what matters most to them, and they're amazingly different in content. Calvin's is full of rocks, leaves, paper notes, and jewelry. Ezra's is full of little bits of toys, coins, and marbles. They store their treasure boxes under their beds, and I see the same air of magic around them as I remember from my own childhood.

Journals

Encouraging your child to journal can be a gift of self-expression that lasts a lifetime. Journaling can begin at a very young age, if you are flexible and creative about how to do it. Remember back to keeping your own childhood diary, if you had one. Wasn't the actual book one of the most important things about it? Guide your children to choosing their own special book to journal in. I'd suggest one with blank pages, particularly for a younger child, where most of the entries will be drawings. Encourage them to journal each day if they want to (by modeling this behavior yourself, of course), drawing pictures and writing words about what they remember from their days and their lives. Share with them some of what you write, of what you define as meaningful moments in your life that you want to remember. Use the journal to write letters that never get sent, to work through big issues in their lives, and to hold on to bits of their lives that matter most to them. A double-sided-tape dispenser can be helpful for attaching bits of paper into the book without glue ruining the pages. As they get older and continue journaling, you'll see their use of the journal change and become an important part of their thinking, processing, and growing. If it becomes important to them, assure them that it is just their private journal, and respect that rule. You'll give them tremendous freedom in doing so—freedom to have their own private space for thinking, art, and dreaming, as well as the ability to see their growth in a concrete, literal way.

YOUR LIFE STORY

Everyone loves to hear and know the story of themselves—the story of how they came to be, what their beginnings in life were like, and how their families began. Making your children a book to tell this story will be a gift they will treasure for a lifetime. As for the subject of the book, that is completely up to you. Some people like to document the time leading up to a decision to start a family; others prefer to start at pregnancy, birth, or adoption. Decide what you want the beginning of this story to be and start from there. We've made a book for each of our children that documents their pregnancy and birth in photographs and words.

Adoptive families can use a life book in a few different ways: a book to document the whole adoption journey, beginning with the decision to adopt or the moment of meeting one another; a photo travel book documenting the adoption trip and process; or a book focused on what the child's life was like before adoption in their birth culture or environment prior to adoption. Depending on what story you decide to tell, the life book for adopted children has the power to educate them about the adoption process, heal feelings of loss, and celebrate themselves and their family. A life book can be a creative way to document, celebrate, and remember any child's "beginnings."

There are a number of ways to make a life book for your child. A scrapbook is quite suitable for this project, as is a photo album with notes. For Adelaide's first birthday, the rest of the family decided to write her a life book by telling the story of her first year. Her brothers decided what would be in the story—her favorite people, places, and things. They assisted in taking photographs (and making quite elaborate staging as well) of such things as our pets, her favorite toys, the beach, and her favorite shoes (this girl loves her shoes). Once the photographs were compiled, the boys then dictated the story to go along with the pictures and addressed it to Adelaide. Next to a picture of her is the caption, "This is you, Adelaide. Sometimes we call you Goo Goo, Baby Goo, Ada, Lady A, or Addie. You have so many names because we love you soooo much." (A little heart swelling, isn't it?) Rather than making a photo album or scrapbook, we chose to put

Adelaide's story into a soft, fabric book, using fabric scraps from the clothing I had made her in her first year. We printed the digital photographs and text (which can be put together in any simple photo software program) onto pretreated fabric that fed through our home computer printer (found at the local sewing shop, you can read a bit more about this fabric in chapter 5, "Creating with Children's Art"). For a sturdier book, I used cotton batting (for quilting) as a middle layer to the pages, which were then all sewn together to create the book's binding.

Whatever method of construction you use, your children will treasure having a book all about them and the beginnings of your family life together!

Adelaide's birthday book, written by her brothers, tells the story of her first year.

9

Everyday Rituals

In dwelling, live close to the
ground. In thinking, keep it to
the simple. In conflict, be fair
and generous. In governing,
don't try to control. In work,
do what you enjoy. In family
life, be completely present.

—Tao Te Ching

I t seems that finding the time is often the biggest obstacle
to creative pursuits. In the busy lives we all have today, it's
a reality that finding the time for creativity might need to
be planned. In the same way that we plan the appointments and self-
care we need in our lives, we also need to plan for the creative projects that are important to us. I believe that having some kind of
active and alive creative spirit is essential to our general well-being.
When creative pursuits are thought of in this way, they become
more than an "extra" and instead become a necessity. Sometimes
that necessity needs to be scheduled to ensure that it will happen.

If you are looking for ways to incorporate more creative time into your lives, these are the two biggest recommendations I have for you:

- *Cut out television.* If you can't or don't want to cut it out completely, then try to cut down how much time you spend watching it (the same can apply to the computer if it's used frequently in your home). Think about the amount of time you and your family spend in front of the television, and how much more you could be doing with that time if you were more active, engaged, alive, and creative.

- *Wake up earlier.* And/or (in my house) go to bed earlier. Good sleep and feeling rested is essential to so much— patient parenting; general wellness; and a fresh, rich creative mind. Be sure that you get all the sleep you need to be at your best. When you've got that time figured out (hard with little ones, I know), try rising a bit earlier than the rest of your family, even if only by a few minutes. You'll be amazed at how refreshing it feels to have a moment or two by yourself in the morning for your own projects (rather than late at night, when you're tired and less energetic). I think you'll be surprised at how much creating you can get done in the morning in a short period of (quiet!) time.

In our hectic age, I think it is ever so important to create and make time for the moments of peace, calm, and ritual in everyday life. These are the special moments when our family is mindfully gathered and fully aware of being in the presence of each other.

Giving our children the ability to find peace and quiet themselves is a tremendous gift. The activities in this chapter are intended to give you more ideas of how to incorporate creative time into your life—not only how to schedule the creative time you need, but also how to creatively spend the time you already have. Finding creative ways to do the things you're already doing can add tremendous joy and fun to your family life. The activities here are also full of ways that you can incorporate creative rituals and togetherness into your family's day-to-day life.

MEETING IN BED

One idea for incorporating creative time into your family life is to have a morning "meeting in bed." A family meeting like this can happen in a variety of ways, and I'm sure you will find what works best for you. For our Meeting in Bed, we all gather on the biggest bed in the house first thing in the morning and begin our official meeting of the minds. Everyone is at the ready with clipboard, paper, and pencil or crayon. We all simply go around and talk about what we would like to get done, projects we want to work on, things we will need help with. Then together (based largely on the ages of the children) we come up with a prioritized list of what's to be done for the day, being sure that everyone gets something they desire on the list.

Some negotiating often needs to happen, and this usually leads to planning even further ahead. The reality is that we are not going to be able to meet every creative desire and wish of our children each and every day, but I believe it is important to find a way to say, "yes" as much as possible. I feel as though every day I'm getting asked for some grand, elaborate, creative plan to be put into action. For example, "Mama, I want to build a tree house today." And with so much else on my mind, so many other people's needs to meet, and a day full of my own plans, the instinctive answer is, "No, not today." But I try as much as I can remember to say, "yes." So my answer becomes, "No, it isn't possible for us to build a tree house today, but *yes*, we can start drawing the plans for one. Then we'll clear a spot, then we'll save money, and the tree house can be built this fall." This not only says a big "yes" of encouragement to their creative desires, but it also teaches them a valuable lesson about creative planning and larger projects.

Of course, in an ideal world, we wouldn't need a list or a schedule for our creative needs to be met. And surely a "family meeting" might not be something that can or should happen every day. However, it can be important in ensuring that we are making time for creating; that we are deciding as a family that creative time is time well spent; and that it's a priority not just when it's convenient, but *all the time*. Once making creative time becomes a priority for your family, it can become second nature, just as making time for family meals or laundry day is. It is choosing to believe and live a life that recognizes creativity as a need and not just a desire.

Don't slip into the habit of relegating your creative projects for "after everything else is done." Work, housework, chores—the lists go on and on, and so does the work. "Everything else" is *never* done. Creating needs to be as important a part of your life as anything else you consider a necessity. There *is* time for creating; you just need to decide to make it a priority for you. If you have to, especially when getting started at incorporating it into your life, you might need to actually schedule your creative endeavors. Schedule them into open spots on the calendar, just as you would an appointment or a meeting. "Making a fort with the kids" really is an activity worth making the time for, and it might need to be put on the calendar next to "Ezra's dentist appointment." The same is true when speaking of your own creative endeavors—make them a priority in your day!

MEALTIME GATHERINGS

For many, the evening meal is a time to gather, to rejoice in each other, and to be grateful for the gifts of each other and the earth from which our food comes. Reminding ourselves at each meal of where our food comes from can tremendously deepen our gratitude and connection to the natural world and to the people we are blessed to share it all with. It only takes a minute or two before beginning a meal to do something to mark the moment. At our home, mealtime rituals, particularly with young children, may only take two minutes, but the effect of them is amazing and so full of life lessons and reminders for all of us. Perhaps you already have your own traditions and rituals, dictated by your history, your religion or spirituality, or your own young family's desires. Here are a few variations of the things we do before dinner.

A Breath

In my home, the few moments before we all sit down to eat are very hectic. Children are full of energy from the day's activities, dinner is being finished up, things are getting moved to the table, and people and spaces are getting cleaned up in preparation for the meal. As a transition to a peaceful, thoughtful meal, we do a family breath once everyone is sitting down. Holding hands around the table, everyone takes a deep breath together, making us all fully present and aware in the moment we are sharing together. It's amazing how clearly the energy changes after a breath—we all slow down, things get a bit quieter, and we're able to fully *see* each other.

Silence

If the breath doesn't work for you, a moment of silence can have similar effects. Sharing a moment of silence together can clear your minds and hearts in preparation for a time of togetherness. Using a meditation bell can be a lovely addition to your family's silent moment.

Holding Hands

We begin our breath by holding hands, creating a circle around our table. This is a powerful way to connect and say "hello" to each other before dinner. After the blessing is said, we often pass a squeeze around the table, as a fun way of ending our before-meal ritual.

Our blessings, written on painted cards, sit in a nature bowl at the center of our table.

Gratitude

Sometimes after a blessing is said, we may express our thanks for something or someone we're particularly grateful for that day.

Often, it's just a thank-you to the cook, which then leads to a round of thank-yous for all the various other things that led to our gathering at mealtime—from the three-year-old who picked up the blocks off the table so we could eat to the farmer who grew the vegetables in our meal. It's a powerful exercise in realizing how many people and how much work go into one simple family meal together.

Blessings

When selecting a mealtime blessing, your religion or spirituality may dictate what you choose to say. You may have a prayer or blessing that you said as a child and continue to say now with your own children. Or your evening blessing may be one that changes each evening to reflect your day. Perhaps it's a song you've always sung or a poem that your children have written. You may say the same blessing at each and every meal, or it may vary with the week, holiday, or season. When our children were quite young, we would select a new mealtime blessing for each new season, providing us with a chance to reflect each night on the changing world around us. At other times, we've kept a bowl of blessings written on cards in the middle of our dining table, with a new blessing chosen each evening.

For the past year now, our family has been particularly fond of a blessing that we adapted from this original version, a traditional blessing commonly used in the Waldorf tradition:

> Earth, we thank you for this food,
> For rest and home and all things good,
> For wind and rain and sun above,
> But most of all for those we love.

Here are some other favorite traditional blessings:

> Blessings on the blossom,
> Blessings on the root.
> Blessings on the leaf and stem,
> Blessings on the fruit.

> For the golden corn and the apples on the trees,
> For the butter and the honey for our tea,
> For fruits and nuts and berries that grow beside the way,
> For birds and bees and flowers,
> We give our thanks today.
> Blessings on our meal and our family.

Art Placemats

These placemats can be such fun to make with even the youngest children. Make enough for everyone sitting around your family table, or make more as gifts.

What You'll Need

- Two pieces of cotton canvas fabric, measuring 18 × 14 inches (Cotton canvas can be found at your local fabric store. Alternatively and inexpensively, you can use a drop cloth, found at your hardware store, as the canvas.)
- Acrylic paints and brushes
- Sewing machine, thread, needle, scissors

Calvin's piece of art—for eating on.

What to Do

1. One piece of the canvas will be your blank painting canvas. With the acrylic paint and brushes,
   you and your children can paint any design or
   picture you'd like on the front (facing side) of
   your placemat.
2. Allow the paint to dry according to the manufacturer's directions.
3. Once dry, place the painted fabric piece on top of
   the second piece of fabric, right sides together
   (the painted side is a right side).

4. Sew around the edges of the canvas mat, leaving a 3-inch opening on one side.

5. Pull the placemat through the opening, so that it is right side out.

6. Smooth out corners and edges and iron flat.

7. Using a straight stitch or a decorative stitch on your sewing machine, topstitch along all four sides, approximately ½ inch from the outside edge, being sure to catch the 3-inch opening.

8. Dine away on your new placemat! Depending on the paint you've used, it might need to be spot cleaned only. Read the manufacturer's directions on the paint you used for information on cleaning.

BEDTIME BAGS

There's no cozier time of day in the life of a child than that moment when you slip into your comfortable pajamas and climb into bed with a favorite story to read. As a parent, it's also one of my favorite times of day that I look forward to and will always remember as being full of snuggling with my little ones.

In addition to needing extra storage space for clothing in my children's bedroom, I also wanted to find a way to make searching for their pajamas easy on their sweet, tired evening selves. Often, after a day full of work and play, it becomes just one more thing to find pajamas and the nighttime story. We came up with Bedtime Bags as a way to keep the pajamas and bedtime story together, handy, and in their own special storage spot. Hung on hooks on the end of my boys' beds, the bags contain all they need for their evening snuggle and read.

If you're not a frequent sewer, don't be intimidated by the thought of making a bag. These basic tote bags are easy and can be made by an older child or an adult. I've given instructions for sewing with a machine, but if hand sewing is your preferred method (or if a very young child is interested in making one), the pattern can be adapted for that as well. It is for a basic, unlined tote bag, but if you are a more experienced sewer, adding a lining and a pocket can be nice touches.

Ready for an easy evening transition, these bedtime bags hold pajamas and a nighttime story.

What You'll Need

- Fabric for the tote, measuring approximately
  38 × 16 inches (Any type of fabric suitable for
  a home sewing machine is okay. I prefer making
  this bag in a cotton weight.)
- Two pieces of fabric for the tote handles, both
  measuring approximately 19 × 4 inches (You can
  use cotton webbing as an alternative.)
- Matching thread, scissors, pins, scissors, sewing
  machine, ruler

What to Do

1. Fold your large piece of fabric in half lengthwise
   with right sides together, so that it measures
   18 × 16 inches.
2. Using the fold as the bottom of your bag, sew a
   straight stitch $5/8$ inch in from the outside edge
   on the two sides of the bag, leaving the top open
   (see illustration A).
3. Turn the bag right side out. Fold the fabric at the
   top open edge of the bag toward the inside, making a folded edge approximately 1 inch down.
4. Machine stitch this fold down, at just less than 1
   inch, through both layers of the fabric.
5. Take your long handle pieces of fabric and fold
   them in half lengthwise. Press with an iron.
6. Open the fold back up, and working lengthwise,

fold the top edge to the middle, where the fold was created. Press. Do the same from the bottom to the middle fold. Press again (see illustration B).

7. Fold both short ends of the handle in approximately 1 inch and press.

8. Following the original fold, fold the fabric in half again, so there are now four layers of fabric together.

9. Stitch along the edges of both long sides of the handle.

10. Repeat for the second handle.

11. Pin the handles to the outside of the tote bag, with folded edge facing in. Place each handle approximately 4 inches in from the side of the tote.

12. Sew handles to tote, making a 1-inch X to secure it.

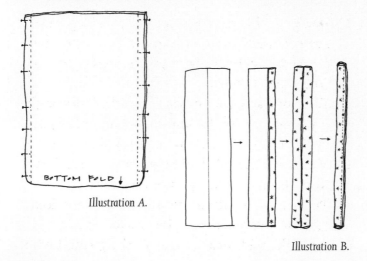

Illustration A.

Illustration B.

part four

Connecting

10

Celebrating Your Family

The child must know that he is a miracle, that since the beginning of the world there hasn't been, and until the end of the world there will not be, another child like him.

—Pablo Casals

Ritual, tradition, and celebration are all very important to me and the way my family marks the milestones in our lives. From what I see around me, I am not alone in the desire to remember and preserve old family traditions and to create new ones. Perhaps it is our current cultural energy of rushing about, with little time for the daily traditions and rhythms that were so much a part of our past; perhaps it is the way in which the generations before us have tossed aside the traditions of their childhood; or perhaps it is our own childhoods, which may have been full of plenty of toys, parties, and material wealth but lacking in tradition and ritual. Whatever the reason, it appears that many of us are looking for ways to celebrate that are creative, affordable, and heartfelt, and that in turn create new traditions for our families.

I shared the activities in this chapter in the hope that they can give you some starting points for incorporating more celebration, tradition, and ritual into your family life. You'll find ideas on celebrating the beginnings of families, as well as the major life events of a child and the magical celebration of birthdays. Here's wishing you much family celebrating!

FAMILY CELEBRATIONS

Oh, the many reasons to celebrate in a family. In addition to the everyday rituals and the seasonal and holiday celebrations, there are also plenty of other reasons in between—surprise events, developmental milestones, and marks of independence. A new job, the first day of school, a half-birthday, the last day of school, potty training, a success at school or on the playing field, an educational highlight, learning something new, taking the training wheels off a bike, the impending birth of a sibling—just to name a few.

If finding more ritual and tradition is something you want more of in your family, consider somehow marking and celebrating these important events with your children. They aren't situations that usually require a grand celebration or party, just little things that send a message of love and connection to your children. Most likely, you have certain rituals in these situations that you don't even realize you have—it's just tradition. Bringing them to the front of your mind can help voice and reaffirm what your family traditions are for yourself and your children, as well as help you reevaluate what you want for elements in your celebrations. Following are just a few examples of the ways in which our family, and families that we know, celebrate those everyday but very special events.

Feasting

Food is the first thing that comes to mind for most people when they think of celebrating. A mindfully and specially prepared meal fills not only our stomachs, but our hearts as well. We feel cared for, loved, and celebrated when someone makes something special just for us. In our home, a special event might be marked by something as simple as baking a cake and having a special dessert after dinner. Or choosing a meal full of the one-to-be-celebrated's favorite things— even if that means a meal of cheese, crackers, kiwi, and french fries.

Special Plates

In some homes, there are the everyday dishes and then the special ones that are reserved for holidays and parties. Marking a family celebration might be as simple as using those special plates on the first day of Papa's new job or Ezra's first bike ride without training wheels. It doesn't need to be anything elaborate, just this tiny little touch of something extraordinary and special is a wonderful way to make the day and the celebrated event stand out as remarkable. Sparkling cider in "fancy" glasses for little ones or beautiful linens on the table. Small, subtle, and very special.

Toasting

Similar to the element of feasting, there is the tradition of toasting. For children and their achievement to be the subject of a toast can be quite a marvelous treat and a sweet way to mark a celebration in your family. Don't forget the clinking of the glasses at the end—the very best part of all. Some children might like to make the toast themselves, as a sort of "announcement" to their family of their achievement—which will, of course, need to be met with cheers, toasts, and "hip hip hoorays" from the family crowd.

Verses

Often, when there is a transition happening in our family—someone moving from the family bed into their own, another beginning their first class without a parent present, or even just a particularly noticeable stretch of peace among siblings—I'll find some words to share with the children to subtly and quietly celebrate the occasion. This usually means looking for a poem that abstractly fits what we are celebrating and reading it before our evening meal or bedtime. It gives us all a moment to pause and reflect individually on the circumstances. Often, there is a conversation that follows about the poem's meaning or relevance in our own lives.

Sharing the News

This is probably one that happens in your home, without actually naming it as such. Especially when I think of the "firsts" in our lives—reading, bikes without training wheels, using the potty, and so on—all of these are met with initial jubilation followed by a phone call to Grammie. These special phone calls give my little ones the chance to share their jubilation and story with one of their favorite people and someone who they know will hear their story—whatever it may be about—with equal enthusiasm and pride. Perhaps there is someone special in your child's life with whom they want to share the news, or perhaps there's a whole phone tree of people who are called when these special things happen. Whichever the case, sharing the news with those we love is the first thing we do as adults to celebrate, and it's only natural that our children should want to celebrate in the same way. In addition to making phone calls, letters can be written, newsletters made for "distribution," and other sorts of "announcements" created for your children to share their special news.

By the Light of the Fire

Fire is one of the most common elements of celebration in families and cultures around the world and throughout history. Gathering around a fire evokes feelings of ritual and tradition and brings us closer to nature and the earth, as well as those standing near us. Bonfires are a magnificent, fun, and sometimes quite powerful way of celebrating, if they are reasonable and accessible to your situation. But you don't need a bonfire to get this same feeling; lighting a fire in your woodstove, fireplace, or outdoor fire bowl can carry the same feeling of ritual and magic. Fire is a wonderful way to celebrate the end of one thing and the beginning of another. If it fits for you and your children, perhaps adding something to fire that represents what you are saying good-bye to can be wonderful. Even writing things down on a piece of paper, tossing it in the fire, and watching it turn into ash can be quite moving at any age. In our home, when we are struggling with leaving something behind or are having lots of fear, this is one way we try to let go of those fears—by writing them down on a piece of paper and tossing them into the fire. There's something freeing and powerful about such an activity, and I've seen even the youngest children be drawn into this experience.

Henna Art for Celebrating

Henna (also called "mehndi body painting") is a traditional art of painting the body with paste made from the leaves of the henna plant. Exactly where mehndi art came from (though the plant is from the Middle East) is debatable, but it has been used for nearly five thousand years as an important element of many rituals and traditions. It is believed that henna was used on pregnant women to decorate their bellies with beauty to "distract" them during birth, as well as on the hands of those about to be married. Today, many women are using henna as part of their birth blessings, and it is also gaining popularity as a decorative art for everyone. I particularly like henna as a way to mark a celebration of any kind—it's a fun activity to do with others and just right for children.

A plant derivative, henna is nontoxic and safe for children, making it a wonderful art form to use as a family. Henna kits are readily available at your local whole foods store and at some craft supply stores, but it can be fun to make it yourself too. There is a wide variety of recipes available online, but here's a basic recipe that I use. Keep in mind that it's relatively different each time you make it, depending on the henna and its consistency, the air temperature where you are, and so forth. You needn't be afraid to experiment a bit to find what makes the best henna mixture for your circumstances.

Henna art by Calvin, age six.

What You'll Need

All of these items can be found at your local natural foods store.

- Black tea (in a teabag)
- Eucalyptus essential oil
- Approximately 1 cup henna powder (The fresher and higher quality the powder, the better color you'll have. Look for fine, talclike, green powder.)
- 1 tsp. lemon juice
- 1 tsp. ground cloves

What to Do

1. Boil 2 inches or so of water in a saucepan. Take the pan off the heat and add the black teabag to infuse for several hours.
2. Add a few drops of eucalyptus oil and allow to infuse overnight.
3. Heat the mixture to a warm temperature, then slowly add it to a bowl of henna powder and ground cloves, stirring with a wooden spoon. You may not need to use all of the water. You want a thin paste, about the consistency of yogurt.
4. Add lemon juice, then add more of the water mixture until it resembles the consistency of toothpaste.

5. Transfer the paste to a plastic bag, in which it can
   be stored for up to two days. Leftover paste can be
   frozen, though I've had mixed results doing so.

Choosing a Design

There are no rules about what to paint. If your children are
participating, keep the designs simple and easy to draw. Decorative lines, flowers, and celestial themes are all favorites
among the children I've done henna with. If you are looking
for more traditional henna art, look online for inspiration, as
well as in books on mehndi art. See illustrations A and B for
samples of henna designs to get you started.

Illustration A.

Illustration B.

Applying the Henna

There are a variety of application methods to choose from. Application bottles are available at craft supply stores, but a more available method to start with is a cone (think of the icing bags used for icing a cake). I prefer working with an icing bag fitted with a very small metal decorating tip. If that isn't available, you can make your own with a strong freezer bag by cutting a very small tip off one of the corners and being sure the henna is sealed in at the top. Tape can be used to reinforce the bag as needed. You'll squeeze the henna out the small tip, just as you would with frosting. You can also use the tip of a paintbrush to paint the paste on, but there is much less control, meaning the lines will be thicker. This method might be best for small children, as trying to make fine lines and small detail may be frustrating for them. Once you've got the henna prepared and in an applicator of some kind, it can be applied to the body as follows:

1. Wash the surface of the skin to be painted, making sure that all dirt, lotions, and oils are removed.

2. Apply a tiny amount of eucalyptus oil to the area to be painted. This will hold the art longer.

3. Using whatever method of application you've chosen, apply the henna to the skin.

4. The henna will dry partially in a short period of time, but try not to touch it much until it is fully dry, which can be up to a half-hour. The henna paste will fall off on its own, leaving the paint behind on your skin.

5. Once it is completely dry, after approximately 4 hours, the rest of the paste can be brushed off, and the skin can now be washed.

6. Depending on the strength of your henna, the art can last anywhere from days to weeks. To hold the color longer, use care when washing the area, putting lotion over it when bathing or getting it wet. On the other hand, if you would like to remove the henna sooner, wash it often.

BIRTHDAYS

I'm sure you agree that a child's birthday is at the top of the list of reasons to celebrate. We're all used to the ideas of a big party, presents, balloons, and cake, but here are a few ideas for some creative new ways to celebrate birthdays in your home. These ideas are centered on celebrating the child and *who* they are, with a little bit less focus on *what* they want and/or have. Following the celebratory ideas are two patterns for special birthday treats for you to make.

Birthday Garden

Why not celebrating your little one's birthday by nurturing the earth in their honor? Dedicate a special spot in your yard as "Ezra's Garden," and this can be the spot where each year you plant a new plant, tree, or flower for his birthday. Children will love having a special spot just for them, and as they grow older, they will enjoy being a part of the process of planting, tending, and playing in their Birthday Garden.

Love Letters

On their birthdays, both my husband and I write "love letters" to the birthday child. Choosing or making a special card that reminds us of them, we each write our own separate letter to be kept for a later age. We write about the memories of the past year or the things we treasure dearly about the child at that age. Bundled together in a special box, I hope they'll someday serve as a reminder of who they were and, most importantly, of how very much they were and are always loved by us.

Birthday Blessings

We have a tradition in our home that we use during birthday cake time. After the candles have been blown out and while the cake is being cut and served, we each say something that we love about the birthday child, something we remember from the past year or something we wish for their coming year. We go around the table, basing the number of blessings on how many years old the child is. So for a first birthday, we'll each give one birthday blessing; on the second birthday, we each give two blessings; and so on. We haven't hit the teen years yet (and the adults are limited to just one blessing), so I don't know how this will change. It might get quite fun going around numerous times, or perhaps the tradition will evolve into something else.

Birthday Crown

This is a very special crown just for birthdays to make the birthday someone feel extra special. A birthday crown is something that can grow with the child and be kept the same or added to each year with minimal sewing required. My children's birthday crowns are among their most treasured possessions.

Made for her first birthday, Adelaide's birthday crown will be worn for many birthdays to come.

What You'll Need

- Wool felt, approximately ½ yard (I prefer 100 percent wool felt or a wool/polyester blend. Both are thicker than the standard polyester felt you might remember from your own childhood craft days. See the Resource Guide for assistance in locating this type of felt.)
- ½- to 1-inch elastic, 5 inches in length
- Needle, scissors, thread, and pins for holding the crown in place
- Embroidery floss, beads, scrap pieces of felt, buttons, and so on for decorating the crown

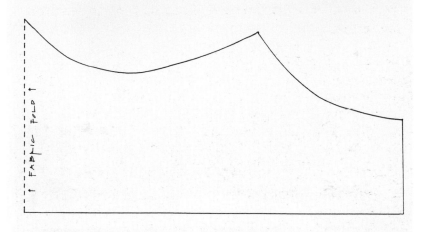

↑ FABRIC FOLD ↑

Illustration C, shown here at 50 percent.

What to Do

1. Following the template (see illustration C, shown at 50 percent), trace and cut out two pieces of felt. One of these will be the front, and the other will be the lining.

2. Decorate the crown front as you wish. I like to embroider or appliqué additional pieces of felt on it. For Calvin's birthday crown, I sewed on a simple yellow star and add another each year. When you are satisfied with the crown front and it's dry (if you're using glue to attach anything), you can move on to the next step.

3. Lay the lining on the back of the crown front and pin in place. Insert the elastic from one side of the crown to the other side on the small "flap" sides, in between the two felt pieces. Pin that in place as well.

4. Begin sewing your crown together. This can be done by hand or by machine. You can use a straight stitch, a blanket stitch, or whatever you like and are able to do. When stitching over the elastic band, be sure to use extra stitches to reinforce it.

5. Crown your special birthday person and begin the celebration!

Birthday Garland

This garland, or "bunting" as it is also called, can really be used at any time of year. It can make a whimsical decoration for a child's bedroom or an accessory to an outdoor playset. Made in various seasonal colors, it can be part of your seasonal or holiday decor. We like to use ours as an alternative to the disposable crepe paper for birthday celebrating. These instructions will make a garland approximately 6 yards in length.

A fabric garland makes a wonderful, reusable birthday decoration.

What You'll Need

- Approximately 2 yards of fabric in assorted patterns and prints
- 6 yards of extrawide double-fold bias tape, found at your local fabric store
- Scissors (Pinking shears are preferable to prevent the bunting from fraying.)
- A sewing machine
- Thread to match the bias tape

What to Do

1. Cut the fabric in triangles to your desired size, using whatever combination of fabrics you would like.
2. Depending on how you want to use your garland and whether the back sides will be viewed or not, you can cut another set of triangles and sew them together (right sides out) along the two long sides of each triangle. If you decide to do just one piece of fabric per triangle, keep in mind that the back of the garland will show the wrong side of the fabric. I use this option when the garland will be used temporarily or as an outdoor decoration (every outside circus tent needs a bunting, don't you agree?).

3. Once you have your triangles completed, gather a pile of them next to your sewing machine. Sew approximately 4 inches of your bias tape closed (this will be the end that gets tied or pinned to something). Open the tape on the fold, place the bottom of the first triangle within the fold, and sew a straight stitch (or a decorative one) to secure the triangle to the tape.

4. Continue to insert the triangles until you reach the end of your tape, leaving a 4-inch end for tying or hanging.

5. Hang your bunting with tacks or by tying it where it needs to be. Let the celebrating begin!

A VISIT FROM THE TOOTH FAIRY

Many people believe that the act of losing baby teeth carries much significance in a child's life. In the tradition of Waldorf Education theory, the age at which a child begins to lose teeth is the beginning of a new phase in their life. It marks the beginning of a developmental phase of being more "out" in the world and more curious about the things around them. In my own experience, the ages of six and seven seem like a tremendous time of change, a time when children need to express themselves individually. Losing teeth seems to be the body's way of making this change, of shedding a layer of its own skin, so to speak. Marking this time in a child's life with something besides the traditional monetary reward can be a wonderful way to celebrate this change.

The Seed Bunny by Jennifer Selby is a delightful children's story about a bunny who gets a special delivery of a packet of seeds when his first tooth is lost. What a wonderful gift! A packet of seeds—a gift that grows, gives, and encourages children to nurture the earth and see what it provides for us.

In preparation for the first tooth falling out, making a tooth pillow can be an exciting project for a young child to anticipate the coming event. A pocket can be placed on the outside of the pillow for a seed packet to go in. I like the idea of giving the child something special to hold and keep their tooth in as well, perhaps a small drawstring bag or a tiny jewelry box. This bag or box can be slipped inside the pillow's pocket.

What You'll Need

- Two pieces of cotton fabric, measuring whatever size you would like your pillow to be (I've made mine approximately 8 inches square.)
- Scissors (Pinking shears can be used to keep the fabric edges from fraying.)
- A sewing machine, if the pillow is to be made by machine
- A hand-sewing needle
- A piece of felt for the pocket, measuring approximately 6 inches square if you are making an 8-inch pillow (Adjust the size as you like.)

- Whatever you wish to use for embellishing the pocket, such as additional felt, embroidery, patches, flowers, and so on
- Stuffing (I prefer using wool or cotton, but any craft stuffing will work.)
- Dried lavender, mint, or rosemary for a scent inside the pillow (optional)

What to Do

1. Embellish the felt piece that will be the pocket as desired. Some children might like to embroider their initial, name, or the word *tooth* on it. Or they might prefer sewing on another piece of fabric, ribbon, or craft flower.
2. Machine or hand stitch the pocket to the right side of one of the pillow pieces.
3. For hand sewing: If you can cut the edges of the fabric pieces with pinking shears, and particularly if your young child is doing this part themselves, you can place the two pieces of fabric with the wrong sides facing. Sew the sides of the pillow together, leaving a 2-inch opening on one side for stuffing.
4. For machine sewing: Place the two pieces of fabric with right sides facing, and sew around all four edges of the pillow, leaving a 2-inch opening on one side for stuffing. Turn pillow right side out.

5. Stuff pillow to desired firmness. Adding a bit of
    lavender, rosemary, or mint to the stuffing can
    make the pillow extra nice for sleeping with.
6. Close the opening by hand stitching.
7. Wait, wait, wait for that tooth to fall out, then get
    the seeds ready!

11

Handmade Holidays

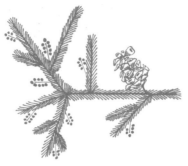

Since you get more joy out of giving joy to others, you should put a good deal of thought into the happiness that you are able to give.

—Eleanor Roosevelt

At the time of year that is most full of the consumption, marketing, and consumerism, I find an overwhelming need to create moments and objects of ritual, creativity, and connection. In the midst of all the shopping and busyness that goes on around me, I feel full of a need to slow down, be mindful, and create with intent and purpose with my children. I strive as a parent to keep our holidays simple; meaningful; and full of love, family, gratitude, and creativity. We work to make as many of the gifts we give as we can. This means that gifts are homemade and simple, but full of intent and loving energy for the people receiving them. When we make gifts for the people we love, we are able to think about them while doing so, and I believe that energy is received and loved in turn. We also try to keep our holiday decorations, celebrations, and events simple and natural, focusing on the gifts that the earth gives us year-round.

The holiday season provides us with an endless number of opportunities for creating with our children—and for instilling in them a love for handmade items. The activities in this chapter will give you just a few ideas on making holiday gifts for the ones you love, keeping the holiday celebration in your home full of creativity, and giving beyond the doors of your home to your community.

A CHILD'S WONDERLAND

There aren't many things more magical to a child than the lights, decorations, and warm feelings that come with the holidays. I remember the feelings of wonder I felt as a child, watching as what seemed like the whole world was transformed into a magical, holiday, winter wonderland. Now as a parent, I've had the joy of watching that sense of magic and wonder appear in my own children's eyes as the holidays approach. While the fancy, elaborate decorations that we marvel at are amazing, just as amazing to me are the signs of a creative childhood during this time. Paper snowflakes covering the windows, paper garland chains hanging from the doorways, and Santa beards made out of cotton balls are all signs of children creating a bit of their own holiday wonder.

This holiday season, I watched my five-year-old son, Calvin, as he fully dove into the project of making his very own Winter Wonderland village. He spent countless December hours dreaming up the plans for his village; laying it all out; gathering bits and trinkets to include; and making new things out of clay, paper, and anything else he could find. It was never "done," but rather became an ongoing creative work in progress that belonged only to him. When he wasn't making things for it, he would gaze into it and "try to imagine a way to get inside the village." It became a creative expression and a form of creative play as well.

When the holiday decorating bug hits your home, don't forget to carve out some space for the little ones to work their own holiday magic. Consider dedicating a prominent spot in your home that your children can decorate as they wish, and provide them with a few things to use. Holiday decorations are found inexpensively at thrift stores or, even better, in your attic. You don't need a large space to make this happen. Calvin's Winter Wonderland was all on top of a dresser in his bedroom that was cleared for the month. Surely a bookshelf, end table, dresser, or other spot can be found in your home if your little ones are interested in creating their own Winter Wonderland or village. This can be a wonderful way for them to feel included in the decorating of your home and a chance for them to share their creative ideas about the holidays.

Friends gather round the Solstice fire for warmth and some marshmallows in Calvin's Winter Wonderland village.

A GIFT TO THE EARTH

In our desire to keep the holiday spirit of giving to all, including those beyond the doors of our home, we began giving a Gift to the Earth. Each year, we've chosen a different gift related to a different issue that we wanted to address. With that gift, we make a yearlong commitment to continue giving. For example, one year, Calvin was just beginning to notice, inquire, and have much sadness about the homeless people we would encounter in our town. So for that holiday season, we decided our Gift to the Earth would be a gift to the people of the earth, the people who had no homes of their own. This gift began during the holidays with an initial donation of a small amount of money, in addition to a box full of things that our local homeless shelter needed—nonperishable food, new blankets, and a few winter coats. Our gift continued through the year, as we made a commitment to ourselves and the local shelter to put together a small box of similar items each month and make as much of a donation as we could. At only three years old, we felt Calvin was too young to participate in helping at a soup kitchen, so we kept our gift to a drop-off that he was able to be a part of. It was an amazing experience for us to commit to a year of giving, and I believe that it gave Calvin's young mind and heart some ease and comfort, knowing that he was doing something, when he saw homeless people in our community. He remembered the blankets, he remembered the canned food, he remembered the drop-offs—and it all made him feel very good whenever we talked about it.

In other years, our commitment has been stronger or weaker, depending on the events in our lives. But we strive each year to work on this Gift to the Earth and hope that it becomes a tradition and ritual that our children will carry on into their adult lives. Following is a list of ideas that your family can use and adapt to give your own Gift to the Earth:

Calvin helps his Grampie clean a walking trail, as a Gift to the Earth.

- *People of the earth*—You can try giving time to a soup kitchen, making donations, or dropping off items shelters need.
- *Trees*—Dedicate yourselves to a year of random tree planting. Contact your city or town to find out how you can help in neighborhood planting. Commit to participating once a month.
- *Adopting a trail*—Do you have a favorite trail or walk in your neighborhood? Commit yourself to caring for it for a year. Bring trash bags along on your walks and pick up the garbage that you see. Clean up the fallen tree branches after storms and pick up brush. Find out if you can help with pruning and/or planning a park. Contact

your local land trust or conservation organization to find out what their needs are.

These experiences and gifts not only provide help to the people and planet we share, but also give our children amazing growing and learning opportunities. Imagine the powerful effect of our children growing up and giving Gifts to the Earth by habit. Surely, it will change our world.

GIVING HANDMADE

There's no shortage of ideas when it comes to what to make for holiday gifts, and I'm sure you and your children have plenty of ideas yourselves. Around the holidays, the inspiration is overflowing from everywhere—craft fairs, the Internet, online craft forums, craft magazines, and craft stores. If you need inspiration, seek these places out to find projects that will be fun for your family to make and give. I've included a few ideas here that you hopefully haven't thought of yet or that might spark your interest to do something else.

Card Sets

This gift is fun and doable for even the youngest in our families. To make a standard 4 × 6-inch greeting card, we fold a piece of 8 × 12-inch heavyweight card stock in half. The children or I then paint, draw, or write messages on the front of the cards, leaving the inside blank, and putting a small signature on the bottom of the back of the card. I purchase envelopes of matching size and color in bulk. So that it doesn't become an intense labor effort, I usually spread this activity out over the year, making a few cards at a time here and there, so that by holiday time, we have a generous stack of them ready to give as gifts. I bundle the cards and matching envelopes up in sets of four or so, and wrap with twine or a pretty string. I then place them in vellum envelopes, and they're ready to go. The recipient can use the cards throughout the year and remember the art of the children they love.

Coloring Books

With the most basic of drawing abilities, you can make handmade, special coloring books for the children you love. Using a standard 8 × 11-inch piece of white paper and a thick, black pen or pencil, create simple designs, patterns, and whimsical drawings for little ones to color in. If you have a high-quality printer/copier, you can copy these drawings onto thick copy paper or have them copied at a print shop. The images can be random, themed, or things that are particularly special to the children who will receive them. Create a colorful page for the cover. When you have enough pages to put together a small coloring book (I generally do fifteen or so), the drawings can be bound at your local print and copy shop. What a joy it will be for a little one to have a special coloring book made by someone they love, and what joy it will be for you to see how they create on top of your creation!

Joy Jars

A Joy Jar is a special jar you can go to when a little bit of extra goodness is needed. They're made quite simply with a recycled or purchased jar that can be decorated with sequins, trim, ribbon, fabric, beads, or anything else you may think of. Inside the jar are strips of paper with a bit of joy written on each one. Write the joyful text with the recipient in mind, with the intention of making them smile. For example, the Joy Jar that Calvin made for his grammie includes the following messages:

- I love it when you call me your angel.
- Think about how much fun it is to sit on the dock at camp.
- I love to go visit Grampie at the fire station with you.
- You make the best toast ever!
- You have pretty eyes.
- You have *so* many fun shoes, Grammie!
- Let's go to the bakery together soon and share a cookie!

These Joy Jars are literally brimming with goodness intended to bring your loved ones pleasure. They are gifts that children of all ages can make, with even the youngest dictating the statements to an adult.

I remember making a Joy Jar for my grandmother, Meme, when I was a small child. She kept that jar on her kitchen stove, made a point to always pick something from it when I was around, and to this day, she still has it. It was something that made me feel special as a child and something I know she treasured simply because she loved me so.

When you think of holiday gift giving as a time for you to share something you love—a time to share the fruits of your creative passions—it becomes a very exciting time of year indeed. Whatever your passion may be, there will likely be a way for you to turn it into gifts for those you love and want to share it with.

SUPPORTING HANDMADE

As much fun as it is to make as many of the holiday gifts as we can, it's not always possible or realistic that we'll be able to do this for everyone on our list. When we're not able to make them ourselves, the next best thing is to find something that someone else has made. The holiday season can be a great time to show support for crafters and artists for the beautiful and meaningful work they do. Try skipping the big-box stores, and instead opt for small-run, one-of-a-kind items made by hand by creative people just like you. Affordable arts and crafts surround us; we just need to look in the right places to find them. The following are some ideas to get you thinking about and looking for handmade gifts to purchase around the holidays.

Craft Fairs

The traditional holiday craft fair is still a standard in many communities. Think beyond what you remember from your childhood, and know that as we've aged, so too have the crafters at the fairs. Give your local fair a try, and you might find things that are just what appeals to you. All the while, you'll be supporting and encouraging local artists and crafters in their passions. Bring your children along for inspiration, encouragement, and experience.

Art Shows

In addition to craft fairs, art shows are another place to find handmade goods by your local artists and crafters. Find out if your local art school or college has an annual holiday show or sale, as many do. You'll often find very affordable and innovative art by budding artists at such sales. And it is so valuable for your children to see you supporting young artists and their work.

Online

Taking craft fairs to a whole new level is www.etsy.com, an online shop. Etsy features thousands of crafters and artists, many of whom keep their creative pursuits as a hobby and sell a bit of their work and passion here and there. Etsy is a fabulous place for finding handmade work, as well as an endless supply of creative inspiration. Other similar, crafty boutiques are found all over the Internet and feature arts and crafts made by hand. Search around for shops like this.

While finding handmade goods for the holidays might take a bit longer or require a bit more effort than if you went to a chain department store, the benefits far outweigh the extra work. Not only are you supporting people in the pursuit of their creative passions by buying their work, but you're also gifting your loved ones with something that is truly unique and handmade with intent. All the while, your children are learning lessons about what kind of work and art you value—a win for everyone.

12

Creative Connections

A healthy social life is found only when in the mirror of each soul the whole community finds its reflection, and when in the whole community the virtue of each one is living.

—Rudolf Steiner

L iving a creative life is made all the more fulfilling and rewarding when we are creating with, for, or because of others. Much creative drive is certainly internally driven, but there is such benefit to creating beyond ourselves, beyond our family, and beyond our homes, for our community and the world around us. Connecting with and creating with others can be a powerful and inspiring act, as well as a wonderful gift for our children, teaching them how to connect and share their own passions with others. The activities in this chapter will get you thinking about all the potential creative connections in your (local and global) community and how you and your children can make a difference in the world through your love of crafting.

CRAFTIVISM

There's a growing and beautiful movement of "craftivists" in the world, doing the important and creative work of "craftivism." Quite likely, there are craftivists right in your own community, and you yourself may be one. Craftivism is activism, with crafting as the means by which a social justice or environmental issue is addressed. While the term *craftivism* might be new, the concept is old: people gather together in a common cause, doing what they know how to do best to make change. Throughout history, women traditionally gathered in communities, in the basements of churches, or in someone's barn and created things for those in need of care and support within their community. During World War II, "make, do, and mend" became the motto of women throughout the United States. Today, crafters are united in their desire for world change on issues such as the environment, health, peace, and social justice. The following are a few ideas on how to get involved with the biggest and longest running craftivism organizations. In the Resource Guide, you'll find the websites for each of these organizations, as well as a list with more organizations to match your creative passions and social concerns.

Afghans for Afghans

Afghans for Afghans is a humanitarian organization dedicated to getting afghans, blankets, hats, socks, and sweaters into the hands of people who need them in Afghanistan. The website is full of information on how to get started with the organization, including clear instructions on what they need and will accept, free patterns to use, and more information about Afghanistan. This is a beautiful way to spread a bit of warmth and peace to people across the globe.

Project Linus

This organization is dedicated to creating, gathering, and distributing new "security blankets" to children who are seriously ill or otherwise in need. Project Linus is set up by local chapters, which often hold gatherings to create blankets together. This can be a wonderful way to connect with others who are creating for change in the world. The website for Project Linus can help you find your local chapter, as well as give you more information about the organization.

Caps to the Capital

Falling under the auspices of Save the Children, Caps to the Capital is a program that aims to save infant lives throughout the world with the simple yet profound act of getting knit and crochet caps to those who need them. You can visit the website to find information on what you can make and where to send it.

The Dulaan Project

Dulaan is the Mongolian word for "warm." And that's just what this organization aims for; it sends warm mittens, hats, sweaters, and scarves to the people who need them most in Mongolia. The website includes patterns, photos, and more information on the project.

Craftivism is a wonderful way to introduce children to a life of acting on their beliefs. It's a way for them to be creative and expressive and to share their creativity with others. It's also a practical way for us to see the power of creating beyond our pure enjoyment as we help others and make the world a better place.

HOOTENANNY

Perhaps music is a big part of the creative equation in your home, or perhaps it's something that interests you but you have little experience with it. As with any creative form, I don't believe that you need to be proficient yourselves in order to encourage your children to discover and pursue their own musical interests. We are all musical to some degree or another, and by simply encouraging, supporting, and giving our children access to the "tools" they need, we can help them achieve anything they are interested in. I encourage you to think about the ways in which you make music in your home. Do you have instruments that are accessible and available for everyone in your family to use? A piano that's off-limits doesn't encourage musical exploration, but a basket full of percussion instruments that everyone can pick up and play as they desire will support musical discovery, play, and experience.

A few instruments and some eager musicians are all you need to get your own hootenanny started.

Even the youngest babies enjoy the sound of a rattle or maraca, and they can take part in the music others make. In our family, my husband is a casual, self-taught guitar player, and we have several sturdy drums available for play. Good-quality children's percussion instruments are rather inexpensive and are available with good sound and variety. We have a number of hand drums, including a floor tom, bongos, and djembe, all of which are easy for even our one-year-old to tap away on but are still enjoyable for our adult drummer friends who visit. Smaller children's instruments are readily available, and I encourage you to explore those as your child reaches an appropriate age and interest level. But for a young family, I think that a good-quality drum is a good start. In addition, keep an instrument basket around that includes anything that would be a fun, safe noisemaker, such as whistles, tappers, maracas, harmonicas, recorders, triangles, and shakers, to name a few. These instruments are all perfect for beginners, because they are not complicated to use and success is nearly instantaneous. Sometimes I separate the "extra noisy" and high-pitched instruments (recorder, flute, and cymbals) and keep those in a special place for outside play—or special times when I know I have the patience to hear three screeching flutes on top of the regular family noise!

By keeping basic instruments like this available to your children, they'll naturally discover and play with them as they do with their toys. Don't forget to play with them yourself. These instruments are purely intended to be fun for you and your child. Just make music together. Play, dance, and have fun.

When you're ready to take your show on the road, consider hosting a Hootenanny! Pete Seeger and Woody Guthrie used the term *hootenanny* to describe a group of people gathered for folksinging. As far as my family is concerned a Hootenanny is simply a party with lots of music around. Gather some friends and family for an evening of music play. Invite others to bring their own instruments, and share what you have as well. I'm sure among you there will be some experienced guitarists, banjoists, or drummers who can help add something to the music. But even if that isn't the case, following the children in your group, give it a try, listen to each other, and you will be surprised to find that a rhythm of sorts naturally forms. You're making music. You're making music with your children and in your community. Using music as a common ground to gather people can be a powerful experience to share.

A Banging Wall

If you're not quite ready to go out and purchase instruments, a Banging Wall is a great alternative. As I'm sure is true in your home as well, we love banging on pots and pans around here, and the adults are certainly no exception. So when we saw a "wall of sound" at a local fair, we knew we needed something like it for ourselves. Fun, easy, and inexpensive to create, it's the best kind of toy for the whole family.

Your Banging Wall can be anywhere, depending on how big you want it to be and where you live. It can easily be set up in a yard, on the side of a house, or even in a basement (for the very patient or, at least, earplug-equipped family). If none of those are possible, you could also adapt this for apartment living by making the Banging Wall a stand-alone piece to be kept inside or mounted on a wall. We wanted ours to be freestanding outside. We have a fairly wooded area around our home, so we used small fallen tree logs to create a basic A-frame shape: We made two As with the logs, placed a log on top to connect the two, and attached logs across the side as well. Use what you already have or can find, such as plywood, logs, and other timber. I'd recommend making it big enough so several children can use it at once without danger of getting poked.

Once you've got a sturdy shape established, the fun of collecting the sound makers begins. We dug around our kitchen for items that were no longer in use, then asked the grandparents for their discarded items too. We also took trips to our local thrift shop to pick up some extras. Anything will work: pots and pans, lids, trays, baking sheets, cake molds, graters, metal bowls, big plastic water jugs, and whatever else you come across that sounds good. Be sure to avoid glass or sharp objects. Once you have your sound makers, you can attach them to your frame. Some of our pieces are nailed to the logs, some are screwed on, and some are hanging from rope, depending on how we get the best sound effect, as well as who is doing the handwork.

Our Banging Wall is a draw for all that visit—both the little ones and their adults.

The last things you'll need are drumsticks. We went back into the woods to find ours in the form of fallen tree branches and sticks, but you can also use wooden spoons. We keep a big bowl of the drumsticks at the ready, attached to the base of our Banging Wall.

Now you're ready to make some music! A Banging Wall can be

great fun for children and adults and will be a huge draw for visitors of all ages to your home, as well as quite the conversation piece. It's amazing and often surprising to create music with children; it brings out the inner drummer in all of us. There's no worry of something sounding "right"—it all sounds cool on the Banging Wall, which is fabulous for the confidence of not only the little ones in the group, but the big people too. Each year, you can add a few extra things—new instruments or found wood. It's a mix of musical instrument, toy, and recycled art for your yard that will fast become a place for gathering and musical merriment.

Age Variations

For the youngest toddler in your family, this activity will be pure fun and something that they are able to be a part of creating. Selecting the materials, testing them out for sound, and selecting "sticks" for drumming, all delight a youngster. A slightly older child can also be involved in the construction of the wall. A five-year-old, with supervision and instruction, can hammer a few of the pieces into the wood. And older children can take part by designing the wall and building it themselves.

ART NIGHT

Before our children were born, I read an article by Jon Spayde in Utne Reader about a Bad Art Night that he and his wife hosted. It was about people in a community gathering to create art together—art with no expectations of success and no high standards for results. We hosted our very first Bad Art Night shortly after, and it was a rousing success. "Bad art" does not mean trying to actually create art that is ugly, but rather shedding the expectations of what art "should" be. It means letting go of the idea that something must be perfect or up to a certain standard. It means you are truly creating for the experience, not the product, and that you are fully creating in each moment of your artwork. Since our children have grown, we've changed Bad Art Night to just Art Night, which seems more appropriate for the younger ones among us.

To host an Art Night, all you'll need is some friends and family, a few art supplies, and work space on which to create. Depending on the space you use and how many people you invite, you can use one large table or many different tables throughout the house. If young children are involved, be sure to cover your work surfaces with a drop cloth, tablecloth, or newspaper, if necessary. Then scatter a few different art supplies—crayons, paints, markers, beads, paper, glue, anything you can think of—about on each table. For the hesitant among you, keeping a stack of magazines and catalogs for making collages can be a nice way to ease into creating art. Invite a few friends over, and let the creating begin. Rip, tear, paste, glue, paint, draw, doodle, and don't even begin to worry about making a mess! This is what Art Night is all about: shedding our fears and inhibitions and forging ahead to the good stuff.

Art Night is about creating in the moment and with others. It's about connecting with those around you while in the process of creating. There is no pressure for who among you makes the best art; it is all process-oriented and should be kept fun and light. It can become a powerful way to create with those you love and care about, as well as an amazing way to get to know someone better. The conversations that will occur while you are creating can be as deep, diverse, and real as you want them to be, because when we are connected to creating, we are connected to those around us as well. In a multigenerational Art Night, the benefits are tremendous for our little ones, who can create alongside the adults in their lives. And what adult couldn't use a little inspiration from children?

At your Art Night, it might be fun to have a collaborative project going on all evening as well. You can keep one large piece of paper or wood or whatever type of "canvas" you'd like, and let the guests add whatever and however they'd like to the piece. Collaborative art at its best!

ART/CRAFT SHOW

You might find that with "all this creating" comes "all this stuff." The many creations you and your children produce can fill up a home in no time at all. So perhaps it's time for your very own Art Show, right in your own home. Different than an Art Night, where you and your friends gather to create art, an Art Show is an opportunity to present your children's creations to your friends and family. This can be as low-key or as formal as you'd like, whatever works for your family. My goal has been to have a yearly showing of the work our family has created. This usually consists of drawings, paintings, and other art of the paper variety hung up for display, either in frames or on Art Clips and Art Wires (see chapter 5). On tables, we share our three-dimensional creations. We host a few friends and family, share in some snacks, and view and adore the art and crafts as you would at any art gallery opening. At the end of the show, a piece can be gifted to each visitor at the gallery showing.

The Art Show can be a wonderful way for children to see their progress and the change in their work over a given period of time. Having it all up for display and reflection to be adored by those they love, and who love them, can only encourage them more in their passion for creativity.

Alternatively, an Art Show can be turned into a collaborative Craft Show with other creative families. Gathering in a common, large space, a Craft Show (particularly around the holidays) is a wonderful way for families to share, sell, and connect through their creations. Having space for both the adults and the children makes

the Craft Show appealing to all shoppers and gives the children involved a taste of what selling their goods is like. Your show can be
set up however you'd like financially, but setting at least a portion of
your proceeds aside for those in need is a great benefit and encouragement for those shopping. And it will once again provide your
children with the idea that their creations and passion can carry the
power to touch people's lives.

CREATING WITH FOOD

We've talked about gathering to create with a community of people
based on a shared passion for art, music, and creating. But is there
anything that people unite and connect over more than food? Food
is much more than just something our bodies need; it's something
that our souls need as well. Paying attention to where our food
comes from, knowing (or being) the growers of our own food, and
connecting and helping others with food is a powerful thing. The
following are some ideas to get you thinking about how food can
be one more area of your life in which you can make a difference
for others. Food truly does have the power to be a source for creativity, connection, and assistance. Arm your children with the skills to
participate in all three.

Creative Cooking

This is the simplest place to start. If you've picked up this book, I as-
sume that there is intent and thought put into the food that you feed
your children and yourselves. You may already be using food as another form of creative expression with your children. Give them the
skills to know not only how to cook (as is age appropriate), but how
to experiment and make the food they eat truly unique and special.

From time to time, my children will ask to make their special "concoctions" in the kitchen. These are special creations all their own that consist mostly of a large mixing bowl full of lots of items from our pantry "measured" in and stirred. At young ages, this mix of beans, rice, raisins, and olive oil usually isn't something we actually eat. It's really about the process at this point—the process of "creating" with food and learning the skills of measuring and mixing, all with no expectation besides that of fun. As they get older and become more comfortable in the kitchen, these creations can turn into their first cooking projects. In the Resource Guide, you'll find a list of several good books on cooking with children, including recipes that are especially successful for your young chefs. In the meantime, find ways to include your kids in the daily cooking that you already do. Can they help gather ingredients? Or mix? Or stir? There is usually something that children can do to help with each meal, and encouraging them to do so if they so desire can lead to an early love of creating with food.

Community Supported Agriculture

Rapidly growing in the United States and Canada, community supported agriculture (CSA) is a method of farming, growing, and distributing food within a community. It is often focused on sustainable agriculture, support of farmers, and natural or organic growing methods. CSA organizations work in a variety of ways, but the general idea is that a community of people support their local farm by buying a share in it at the start of the farming season. Throughout the harvest, a weekly pickup or delivery of the goods from the farm is made to each of its share members. Some CSAs also require, or at least encourage, members to participate in the farming process by planting, weeding, and harvesting. Many CSAs also have events, gatherings, and social and educational opportunities for their members to participate in.

If gardening is not possible given your time or space, joining a

CSA can be a wonderful way for your children to see and understand where their food comes from. It also becomes a chance for your family to be involved in the process of growing the food you eat. Knowing where your food comes from is tremendously important, especially to a growing child, and seeing this process in a community sense can have a tremendous impact on their buying and eating choices in the future.

Food as Aid

The need for food and nourishment is the most basic of human needs. There are many ways we can share what we have (and what we have access to) with those who do not have food. I'm sure you can find endless opportunities to do this in your community—through a soup kitchen, your church or social organization, food drives, and more. I encourage you to make a commitment to "share your food" as you are able and to include your children in this process.

Calvin and Ezra search for the ripest of berries at our local community garden.

It's also important to think about the ways in which food can help people in our immediate family and community of friends. Perhaps they may not always need food to satisfy physical hunger, but they may need the good energy from thoughtfully prepared food to fill an emotional or spiritual hunger. The act of baking for someone who "needs" it—however that need is defined—is a tremendous act of generosity that can create warmth and positive change in the lives of those around us. What a gift for children to learn that the end result of their creating with food can have such a tremendous impact on people and the world.

afterword

It is my wish that the activities and ideas you've found in this book will encourage you to incorporate creativity into your family's everyday life. That perhaps you'll now have a bit more confidence in the belief that you have it in you to create—in whichever ways you choose—and just as importantly, that you have it in you to patiently encourage, gently guide, and calmly nurture the same confidence in your children. Embracing creativity as a part of who you are will surely bring more passion, intent, and fun into the lives of your children, yourself, and your family. I wish you much creating happiness!

resource guide

The following books and websites are by no means intended to provide a comprehensive list of resources for each topic. They are, however, favorite resources of my family and ones that I refer to often.
Let's think of it as sharing what's on my bookshelves and in my
bookmarks. I hope this guide can provide you with some inspiration
for your own family's interests and activities, or perhaps a start in
taking a bigger leap into any of these creative activities and pursuits.
Also included here are the sources for the materials referenced
throughout this book.

Finding and Nurturing Your Own Creative Spirit

Gregory, Danny. The Creative License: Giving Yourself Permission to be the
    Artist You Truly Are. New York: Hyperion Books, 2006.
Price, Dan. Radical Simplicity: Creating an Authentic Life. New York:
    Running Press, 2005.
Smith, Keri. Living Out Loud: Activities to Fuel a Creative Life. San
    Francisco: Chronicle Books, 2003.
Yamaguchi, Jeffrey. 52 Projects: Random Acts of Everyday Creativity. New
    York: Perigree, 2005.

Do-It-Yourself/Crafty Revolution

Beal, Susan, et al. *Super Crafty: Over 75 Amazing How-To Projects.* Seattle: Sasquatch Books, 2005.

Berger, Shoshana, and Grace Hawthorne. *ReadyMade: How to Make [Almost] Everything: A Do-It-Yourself Primer.* New York: Clarkson Potter, 2005.

Craftster (www.craftster.org)—A forum for people who love to make things.

Etsy (www.etsy.com)—A place to buy and sell handmade items.

Karol, Amy. *Bend-the-Rules Sewing: The Essential Guide to a Whole New Way to Sew.* New York: Potter Craft, 2007.

Lubelski, Nayu. *The Starving Artist's Way: Easy Projects for Low-Budget Living.* New York: Three Rivers Press, 2004.

Nicolay, Megan. *Generation T: 108 Ways to Transform a T-Shirt.* New York: Workman, 2006.

Railia, Jean. *Get Crafty: Hip Home Ec.* New York: Broadway Books, 2004. (Also contains resources for craftivism.)

Gentle Parenting

Drew, Naomi. *Peaceful Parents, Peaceful Kids: Practical Ways to Create a Calm and Happy Home.* New York: Kensington, 2000.

Kabat-Zinn, Jon, and Myla Kabat-Zinn. *Everyday Blessings: The Inner Work of Mindful Parenting.* New York: Hyperion, 1998.

Napthali, Sarah. *Buddhism for Mothers: A Calm Approach to Caring for Yourself and Your Children.* Crows Nest, N.S.W.: Allen & Unwin, 2003.

Sherlock, Marie. *Living Simply with Children: A Voluntary Simplicity Guide for Moms, Dads, and Kids Who Want to Reclaim the Bliss of Childhood and the Joy of Parenting.* New York: Three Rivers Press, 2003.

Weil, Zoe. *Above All, Be Kind: Raising a Humane Child in Challenging Times.* Gabriola Island, B.C.: New Society Publishers, 2003.

Celebrating Nature with Children

Clark, Delia, and Steven Glazer. Questing: A Guide to Creating Community Treasure Hunts. Hanover, N.H.: University Press of New England, 2006.

Cornell, Joseph Bharat. Sharing Nature with Children. Nevada City, Calif.: Dawn Publications, 1998.

Kane, Tracy. Fairy Houses. Lee, N.H.: Light-Beams Publishing, 2001.

Leeuwen, M. The Nature Corner: Celebrating the Year's Cycle with a Seasonal Tableau. Edinburgh: Floris Books, 1990.

Liles, J. N. The Art and Craft of Natural Dyeing. Knoxville: University of Tennessee Press, 1990.

Louv, Richard. Last Child in the Woods: Saving Our Children from Nature-Deficit Disorder. Chapel Hill, N.C.: Algonquin Books, 2005.

Lovejoy, Sharon. Roots, Shoots, Buckets and Boots: Gardening Together with Children. New York: Workman, 1999.

Petrash, Carol, and Donald Cook. EarthWays: Simple Environmental Activities for Young Children. Beltsville, Md.: Gryphon House, 1992.

Handwork, Craft, and Art with Children

Berger, Petra. Feltcraft: Making Dolls, Gifts and Toys. Edinburgh: Floris Books, 1994.

Cooper, Stephanie, Christine Fynes-Clinton, and Marye Rowling. The Children's Year: Crafts & Clothes for Children and Parents to Make. Stroud, England: Hawthorn Press, 1986.

Davis, Tina. See and Sew: A Sewing Book for Children. New York: Stewart, Tabori and Chang, 2006.

Falick, Melanie. Kids Knitting. New York: Artisan, 2003.

Fryer, Jane Eayre. The Mary Frances Sewing Book. Grantsville, Md.: Hobby House Press, 1999.

Gosse, Bonnie, and Jill Allerton. A First Book of Knitting for Children. West Midlands, England: Wynstones Press, 2004.

Jaffke, Freya. *Toymaking with Children*. Edinburgh: Floris Books, 2003.

Martin, Laura C., and David Cain. *Nature's Art Box: From T-shirts to Twigs, 65 Cool Projects for Crafty Kids to Make with Natural Materials You Can Find Anywhere*. North Adams, Mass.: Storey Publishing, 2003.

Mavor, Salley. *Felt Wee Folk: Enchanting Projects*. Concord, Calif.: C&T Publishing, 2003.

Nicholas, Kristen. *Kids' Embroidery: Projects for Kids of All Ages*. New York: Stewart, Tabori and Chang, 2004.

Activities and Games for Children

Blood, Peter, and Annie Patterson. *Rise Up Singing: The Group Singing Songbook*. Bethlehem, Pa.: Sing Out Publications, 2004.

Emberley, Edward. *Ed Emberley's Drawing Book: Make a World*. New York: Little, Brown Young Readers, 1972. (See all of his other wonderful books as well.)

Kohl, MaryAnn F. *Making Make-Believe: Fun Props, Costumes and Creative Play Ideas*. Beltsville, Md.: Gryphon House, 1999.

Luvmour, Sambhava, and Josette Luvmour. *Everyone Wins: Cooperative Games and Activites*. Gabriola Island, B.C.: New Society Publishers, 1990.

Striker, Susan. *Please Touch: How to Stimulate Your Child's Creative Development Through Music, Movement, Art and Play*. New York: Fireside, 1986.

Creating Food with Children

Katzen, Mollie. *Honest Pretzels: And 64 Other Amazing Recipes for Cooks Ages 8 & Up*. Berkeley, Calif.: Tricycle Press, 1999.

————. *Pretend Soup and Other Real Recipes: A Cookbook for Preschoolers & Up*. Berkeley, Calif.: Tricycle Press, 1994.

Yolen, Jane, Heidi E. Y. Stemple, and Philippe Beha. *Fairy Tale Feasts: A Literary Cookbook for Young Eaters and Readers*. Northampton, Mass.: Crocodile Books, 2006.

Family Celebrations

Carey, Diana, and Judy Large. *Festivals, Family and Food.* Edinburgh: Floris Books, 1986.

Courtlund, Yana, Barb Lucke, and Donna Miller Watelet. *Mother Rising: The Blessingway Journey into Motherhood.* Berkeley, Calif.: Celestial Arts, 2006.

Darian, Shea. *Seven Times the Sun: Guiding Your Child through the Rhythms of the Day.* Phoenix, Ariz.: Gilead Press, 1999.

Fabius, Carine. *Mehndi: The Art of Henna Body Painting.* New York: Three Rivers Press, 1998.

Gosline, Andrea Alban, and Lisa Burnett Bossi. *Welcoming Ways: Creating Your Baby's Welcome Ceremony with the Wisdom of World Traditions.* San Raphael, Calif.: Cedco Publishing, 2000.

Lang, Virginia, and Louise B. Nayer. *How to Bury a Goldfish: And 113 Other Rituals for Everyday Life.* New York: Rodale Press, 2000.

Maser, Shari. *Blessingways: A Guide to Mother-Centered Baby Showers— Celebrating Pregnancy, Birth and Motherhood.* Greenbrae, Calif.: Moondance Press, 2004.

McElwain, Sarah. *Sayng Grace: Blessings for the Family Table.* San Francisco: Chronicle Books, 2003.

Craftivism

Afghans for Afghans project—www.afghansforafghans.org

Caps to the Capital—www.savethechildren.org

Christiansen, Betty, and Kiriko Shirobayashi. *Knitting for Peace: Make the World a Better Place One Stitch at a Time.* New York: Stewart, Tabori & Chang, 2006.

Church of Craft—www.churchofcraft.org

Craftivism.com—www.craftivism.com

The Dulaan Project—www.fireprojects.org/dulaan.html

Project Linus—www.projectlinus.org

Revolutionary Knitting Circle—www.knitting.activist.ca
Warm Up America!—www.warmupamerica.com

Art Supplies and Toys

A Child's Dream (www.achildsdream.com)—Source for plant-dyed,
    100 percent wool felt
Dharma Trading Co. (www.dharmatrading.com)—Source for textile
    paints, freezer paper, clothing blanks, and other craft supplies
Magic Cabin Dolls (www.magiccabin.com)—Source for natural toys
    and art and craft supplies, including wool for use as stuffing
Nova Natural Toys and Crafts (www.novanatural.com)—Source for
    natural toys, art and craft supplies, and play silks
Rosie Hippo's Toys and Games (www.rosiehippo.com)—Source for
    natural toys, games, and art supplies